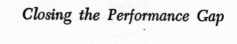

Closing the Performance Gap

ABOUT THE AUTHOR

MARION S. KELLOGG is manager of Individual Development Methods Service in the General Electric Company corporate headquarters. She holds degrees from Manhattanville College of the Sacred Heart and Brown University and has done advanced study at Union College.

Miss Kellogg joined General Electric as a personnel planner and served as personnel placements supervisor, supervisor of technical and supervisory personnel, and manager of employee relations before she assumed her present position in Management Development and Employee Relations Services.

Miss Kellogg is author of *What to Do About Performance Appraisal,* published by American Management Association in 1965.

CLOSING THE PERFORMANCE GAP

Results-Centered Employee Development

By Marion S. Kellogg

American Management Association
New York

FOREWORD

THIS IS A HANDBOOK FOR THOSE WHO GET WORK DONE
through other people—foremen, supervisors, managers,
public and private administrators. Theirs is the task of
deciding what must be accomplished, organizing and putting in place systems to facilitate accomplishment, and
encouraging employees to develop abilities and attitudes
which assure accomplishment. It is to this last requirement that this book is dedicated. It is not restricted to
the development of managers or professionals, but presents principles and practices which apply to all employees.

There has been a tendency in late years to say that
all development is self-development and, having said it,
to avoid coming to grips with the importance of the
contribution managers can make to the growth and career
advancement of employees. Emphasized here, then, are
the basic factors which affect occupational growth—the
work the employee does and the climate in which he
does it as well as his personal talents and motives. But
also emphasized are the specific actions *managers* need
to take to assure a favorable interaction among the three,
one which results in employee development directed toward organization goals and compatible with individual
values.

Involved are three basic and quite different things: *defining* the development results needed from a given individual or organization, *knowing what to do* to obtain

the results, and *wanting* to obtain the results. Each of these areas is explored to understand the nature of the problems likely to be encountered, the truly remarkable opportunities which exist, and the tools and approaches available to managers for solving the one and exploiting the other.

In view of the continuing upward shift in skills required by business and industry, as well as the increasingly higher level of education which is characteristic of today's workforce, managers face a greater and greater need to make use of new concepts and tools as rapidly as they become available. This means that those who seek to contribute to the development of employees—as well as to their own advancement—must undertake self-development programs in order to make the grade. This book is designed to provide the information base for doing just that.

—M. S. K.

CONTENTS

CHAPTER I

EMPLOYEE DEVELOPMENT: A BUSINESS "MUST"

Y EARS AGO COMPANIES ESTABLISHED EMPLOYEE DEVELOPment programs as a "charitable" thing—a part of their human relations effort. It is now becoming obvious that employee development is a part of being in business and that the charity is self-directed.

Entirely new technologies have appeared on the scene, involving new kinds of knowledge, new levels of innovation, and new methods of operation. The resulting demands for scarce talent can be solved, in the majority of cases, only through internal growth. Changes in population—increasing numbers of people, shifts in age distribution, rising education levels—all call for dramatic changes in organization and methods of managing. Economic factors such as the cost-price squeeze and the impact of defense spending on normal commercial businesses and administrative agencies reinforce the need for every institution, public and private, to make full use of employees' talents and to accelerate growth in specific, useful directions.

There is clearly room for improvement here. Almost all employee attitude surveys reveal that employees feel

9

they possess talents they have no opportunity to use. Turnover is high among professionals who give as their reason for leaving an organization that they see no opportunity for personal growth or organizational advancement. Many industrial workers, including even key executives, reportedly are losing their "will to work."

"At a time when the search for all forms of talent and skill is growing more and more intense," says one observer, "it is ironic to reflect that upwards of 90 percent of the capability of every company's present workforce is going to waste."[1] "About 100,000 middle- and upper-management executives will change jobs this year,"[2] predicts a widely read periodical. And still another commentary points to a more insidious form of executive "dropout": "He does not leave . . . yet he has ceased to function as a mover, innovator or contributor to the forward thrust of the company."[3]

While past efforts to encourage employee development have not been entirely successful, it would be totally unfair to imply that there has not been startling individual and organization growth in some cases. Our new businesses and technologies would not be with us if this were not true. There is, however, a widespread feeling among professionals in the field that *development of individual talent has frequently occurred in spite of management efforts* and that systematic approaches to stimulating employee growth have been primarily marked by administrative burdens on line managers, a rapid increase in paperwork, inordinate numbers of meetings called to "plan" action, and very little actual developmental activity other than that initiated by specific individuals for their own benefit.

---

1 Miller, Norman R., "Career Guidance—A Means of Tapping Hidden Potential," PERSONNEL, July-August 1964.

2 *Nation's Business,* August 1966.

3 Beckwith, Lee S., in *Dun's Review and Modern Industry,* April 1966.

"Crown Prince" or *"Opportunity for All"?*

There have been two basic approaches to development, with perhaps an infinite number of variations and mixes. The first is the "crown prince" approach; the second is that of "opportunity for all." In the first, a few individuals are identified as showing outstanding promise of growth and through a variety of techniques are given special attention, subjected to broadening or deepening experiences, and groomed to take over anticipated key assignments. Critics of this sort of system have argued the unfairness to the remaining employees, who, while not excluded from consideration, are in a much less advantageous position in competing for higher openings as these occur. They also point to the harm sometimes done the individual earmarked in this fashion, his feeling that he "has it made" and no longer needs to drive so hard.

On the other hand, opponents of the "opportunity for all" system point to the great amount of effort required to raise the level of contribution for the total workforce and to the fact that not everyone wants or should want to advance occupationally. Let us immediately concede the validity of these objections in many cases—but insist it is possible to devise a mix of the two approaches in an organization setting which minimizes the negative results. Much of the content of this book is, in fact, devoted to the ground rules for doing just this.

Far more devastating, however, is the evaluation of development programs, regardless of type, as *ineffective* by those who have taken a careful look at them from a professional viewpoint. Probably the most time, effort, and funds have gone into the development of managers. But one critic reports:

If enthusiasm and money could insure success, management development programs should be turning out managers enough for all industries. Yet, the evidence is to the contrary. I have analyzed the results of 400 experimental studies concerned with management development and found much disappointment and disillusionment. In many cases, these programs have had little or no demonstrable or measurable effect on business performance or manager behavior.[4]

Now, the academicians may argue whether the results are there but the measuring tools are too blunt to detect them or the results too small for the investment required. The facts are that the time and money investment has been high, the paperwork enormous, and the number of starts and stops and start-over-agains substantial enough to make any student of management question the value received and seek more rewarding systems.

Moreover, when programs have been limited to the upper 5 to 10 percent of employees considered most promising, the record for predicting those most likely to succeed has not been exactly phenomenal. For example:

> . . . repeated, after-the-fact examinations at General Electric and other companies indicate quite consistently that, for all but a few exceptional companies, *less than 30% of the individuals identified as being the leading candidates for a position ever actually achieve it.* Similar kinds of results are found when we examine the histories of individuals who do achieve top-level managerial positions. More often than not, less than one-half of such individuals have appeared on the most-promising-young-men lists early in their careers, or have been paid in the top quartile of their age group.[5]

4 House, Robert J., "A Commitment Approach to Management Development," *California Management Review,* Spring 1965.

5 Ferguson, Lawrence L., "Better Management of Managers' Careers," *Harvard Business Review,* March-April 1966.

If these figures can be accepted literally, it means that about half of those who will rise to top positions in a given company will probably not be included in a crown-prince program at any given point in time.

The Chief Complaints—and Some Remedies

Confronted with any problem for which past solutions have been less than effective, executives normally take some quite specific steps. They examine what they have been doing to determine the probable causes of failure and then systematically adjust their actions, try new approaches, and apply new methods which hold greater promise. To apply this pattern to development programs, what are the chief complaints and what steps might be taken to overcome them?

Overemphasis on information gathering and appraisal. One of the early steps in every development program is an assessment or appraisal of individual ability, career interests, and growth potential. In an effort to make this evaluation as accurate and useful as possible, managers and supervisors are frequently asked to complete elaborate rating sheets concerned with individual performance, work methods, attitudes, personal qualities, interests, and similar factors. Often committees are established or professionals appointed to attempt the reconciliation of appraisal standards among various managers and to document the evidence on which they base their evaluative conclusions. Often, too, planning boards are set up to identify those who most need and are most likely to benefit from specialized development programs.

Except in very small companies, the time which elapses during this stage of the development process is very high, and action is delayed correspondingly. If, meanwhile, there are shifts in organization or work or managers, some reappraisal may be necessary. This slow start, added to the inadequacy of most managers' evaluations, generally produces a negative reaction from top management, intermediate-level managers, and even rank-and-file employees. However impatient they may be, the information-gathering and appraisal stage cannot, of course, be eliminated entirely. We do need all the relevant information available about employees. But greater emphasis can and should be placed on early establishment of development goals, clearly defined at the level of the company and each of its organization components. These goals can then be quickly interpreted and adapted to the individual, thus avoiding excessive start-up delays.

Lack of innovation in planning. Too often, when the development program continues beyond the point of appraisal and development plans are devised, they show, on the whole, remarkably little ingenuity—even though they may be tailored to the individual and his needs and not applied wholesale. Training needs are most likely to be identified, and occasionally another position or series of positions is specified which would add to the individual's exposure and supposedly prepare him for a higher-level job. The recommendations may be sound; they are hardly novel.

Lack of innovation in development planning is usually the result of two factors. The first is inadequate understanding of the development process and ignorance of the wide variety of tools and approaches available to a manager for his personal use in individual cases. The second is the hurried attention to the subject which stems from a feeling that this effort has lower priority than many others and that not much is expected in the way of results. The remedies are almost certainly (1) information and (2) a demonstrated management intention which shows itself in the personal example and reward system of the organization's top executives.

Development which remains an "extra." "Individual A cannot be moved to a planned assignment because his current work requires his full attention for the foreseeable future." "We are simply too busy to hold appraisal discussions now. Will do them after the first of the year." "Why do you pick this particular time for your development program when you know it is the worst time of the year for us?" These and similar managerial comments indicate the extracurricular light in which employee development is viewed. Only an alignment of development needs and work results will minimize the hazard. This means focusing development goals squarely on work commitments, thus giving the manager a powerful additional means for contributing to the success of his organization.

Such a focus has important implications, also, for the individual employee. If he assumes his rightful responsibility for his total personal life, he can no longer seek a job solely on the basis of the particular type of work he may like to do. He must, in addition, be willing to align his personal goals with those of the organization he joins, or he must believe he can influence the organization goals so as to bring them into reasonable agreement with his own. This, in turn, implies an active role in the planning processes of the firm—business as well as developmental—at whatever level he may be working.

Spotlight on the Individual Manager

The remedies we have suggested can be incorporated in a practical way into the work of any company, agency, or other organization by taking these steps:

1. Make work-focused development goals explicit for every employee.
2. Expect every manager to achieve his defined share of the firm's development goals as a part of his normal work.
3. Implement the work of employee development just like other work.

Explicit goals. Regardless of their nature, all organizations have two distinct employee development goals. The first is for every employee in every job to improve his performance: to outperform his counterpart in competitor organizations, to increase the quality and quantity of his output. This is not a "good resolution" kind of goal. If the organization is in business or industry, the pressure of competition forces it. If the organization is nonprofit, demands for reduced costs and increased productivity are the motivating factors.

Employee development also aims at growth to meet the longer-term plans of the organization. This is the second goal. It may mean acquiring new technological or management skills, sounding out new market possibilities, learning new customer habits, expanding geographically. These are not likely to happen by chance. Just as all other assets of the organization must be thoughtfully evaluated in order to arrive at sound plans for the future, so the people assets need to be assessed and plans made for adequate, well-prepared man- and womanpower.

The chief executive needs to make both these goals of employee development explicit; he needs to interpret them specifically for the organization as a whole and to guide their interpretation at successive levels within the company.

Part of normal work. When is work work and not an extra? When it is treated by higher levels of managers *as* work. If managers are repeatedly asked about product improvement and customer response and seldom asked about employee growth in their organizations, they will treat employee development as an extra. If the reasons for failure to meet commitments are always discussed in terms of equipment or vendor deficiencies, unrealistic original planning, or increased competition, managers are unlikely to see the relationship between these problems and individual performance improvement. To make this relationship clear requires a conviction which permeates the thinking and actions of the chief executive and, in turn, influences the attitudes of managers throughout the firm. Simply stated, it is this:

A key factor in success or failure to meet commitments is the extent to which employees as individuals and in association with each other use their talents fully and develop them rapidly enough to meet the organization's needs. To insure this is a major part of the manager's work.

Implementation. Once employee development is seen as part of the results expected from managers, the company—led by its chief executive—can organize to handle it on just as efficient, economical, and effective a basis as other work. This means looking at the total development needs and opportunities implicit in both current and longer-range plans and reaching decisions on those targets which appear to have the most promise. Then the major developmental steps needed to reach these targets can be determined. Responsibilities can be grouped in some sort of logical fashion so as to provide for flow between individuals and organizations; persons can be chosen who will be responsible for major segments of the work; and, finally, follow-up systems can be established for assuring development results and revising plans in the light of current evidence.

If all this is done, the role of every individual in the company's development plans is defined, and it becomes clear that the responsibility for effective development rests with each manager. Not that he *does* the work of development any more than he does technical or sales or purchasing work. But he has an important role to play and a key—if not *the* key—contribution to make.

Isn't this emphasis on the contribution of each manager likely to mean unevenness of effort, talent, and results? Of course. Managers are not equally gifted or equally interested in employee development. This is not a new problem, though—it must be reckoned with in all work. Whenever we depend on others for results, we assume this risk. We minimize it by making certain that each individual knows what is expected of him and, in fact, is involved in the formulation of his work goals and the measurement of his results, that there are adequate resources and facilitating systems available to him, and that accomplishment is recognized and rewarded both consistently and appropriately.

We don't, however, give an individual a job to do unless he has the knowledge, skill, and interest he needs to do it successfully—or can acquire them quickly enough—and it is perhaps in this respect that organizations have most frequently failed when building development programs. Managers, by and large, are not equipped by education or experience for the work of development. They need an understanding of the process, they need to know the company's philosophy, they need to see their role, they need to be sufficiently involved in formulating their share of the expected results. And, thus motivated, they need to acquaint themselves with the wide range of tools and approaches which can help them to achieve those results, and they need the opportunity to develop skill in using them.

The specifics of philosophy, development-goal definition, planning, and implementation, chief executives must supply for their organizations. Personal skill, managers must improve for themselves. To supply the information base for both is the goal of the chapters which follow.

CHAPTER II

UNDERSTANDING THE MANAGER'S RESPONSIBILITY FOR DEVELOPMENT

ASKING MANAGERS AT ALL LEVELS OF THE FIRM TO achieve specific employee development goals is not the same as asking them for a new product or a cost reduction or an improvement in quality. At the very least, managers have seen their associates tackle these latter problems, and much of their academic and company-sponsored training has been directed toward obtaining just such results. True, innovation is possible even here, but the point is that managers are better equipped to face it in these familiar areas.

To meet an employee development goal is quite different. Some few managers have been sufficiently interested in the subject to do considerable reading and thinking on their own or take courses at local institutions. Others, typically, have had the required college-level courses in psychology or sociology (which they may find difficult to relate to current problems) and in-house training in human relations (which even personnel men admit has been notably unsuccessful). Moreover, most supervisors or managers feel they have seen very little in the way of clear-cut, well-labeled developmental action on the part of previous or current bosses; so their ideas about development—what it is and how it happens—are very sketchy. They tend to think of it in terms of preparing individuals for some imagined future position; and, faced with the choice between today's results or someone else's job five or ten years from now, they unhesitatingly choose today's results.

Time, of course, provides the major dilemma. "There simply aren't enough hours in the day to do the immediate essential work," the manager reasons. "As soon as things quiet down a little, I'll think about development." Or, "*Next* year's plans will definitely include employee development." So a sounder, more closely work-related understanding of the development process becomes essential.

Why a Manager Encourages Development

What is development? Very simply, it is a change in the person—a favorable change—that permits him to function more effectively. This change can, of course, be in a variety of directions, not necessarily job-connected. True, change in any direction may have an effect on an employee's performance; however, the organization (as represented by its managers) is primarily concerned with those changes which are directly associated with capacity to perform work. The result of development—the way a manager knows it has occurred —is that the employee possesses new knowledge or information, is able to apply old knowledge in a new way, or has an increased interest in applying what he knows. In other words, he has learned to do something or he has shifted his values.

Four basic concepts clarify the nature of development and provide managers with needed motivation for taking development action. First, the gap between actual and planned results can frequently be erased by viewing it as a development problem and taking specific action of an employee development nature. Managers tend to tackle such a discrepancy as an organization problem, a resources problem, a planning problem, a communication problem—anything but a development problem. Any or all of these may have contributed to the situation; but, on a more fundamental level, it usually represents a personal performance or attitude failure which might have been avoided if the manager involved had done his development homework.

For example, suppose that Manager X finds a product-testing program is lagging behind schedule and asks why. The answer comes back that the paperwork system is so burdensome and time consuming that some of the requests for purchase orders were late and, therefore, needed instrumentation has not arrived. Manager X should ask himself the serious question: "If the paperwork system is burdensome, why didn't someone mention it long ago so that it could have been fixed in time to avert this trouble?" The answer may be that the individuals involved need better planning or follow-up skills or that communications channels are blocked in some way or that employees do not share his concern for meeting the product-testing schedule. These are employee development problems which need his attention. If he solves only the paperwork problem this time, next time it may be the vendor's performance, inadequate cooperation on the part of some other department, or a poorly conceived original schedule which is blamed when the product-testing group is not fully successful. If, on the other hand, he solves the fundamental development problems, employees may be able to take care of new difficulties for themselves.

Second, managers cannot really choose between "doing" development now or later—fortunately or unfortunately as the case may be. Employees grow whether or not the manager puts development activity into his plans. It may not be along the lines the manager, given a choice, would prefer. It may not even be along lines the employee would desire if he stopped to make a rational decision. But, given normal human beings, additions to knowledge and skill occur; interests, attitudes, and values shift in direction and intensity. The extent of change varies with individuals and with their living environment; but they do change and the change means deterioration in some directions, growth or development in others. Let's look at three typical examples.

John Jones is a bright, capable young engineer on a job which every day requires him to learn more about light-weight mechanical design. The work problems he faces are not solved in any textbooks. They require contact and discussion with some of the leading materials men in the country. They require some extrapolation of old ideas, some new ones, a great deal of trial and error. Always provided he has the basic talent and interest to rise to the challenge, John's daily growth along creative technical lines is likely to be high.

Mary Smith is a secretary. When she first came to work for her present boss, the fact that he dictated a great deal and at a very high speed was a great challenge to her. It meant she had to improve her shorthand and transcription skills if she was going to keep her job. After two years, however, these skills are second nature to her; the job has settled into a routine; and, because there is already a high volume of work, little new responsibility has been added. Mary could look for another job, but this is a very comfortable one and, instead, she becomes interested in little-theater work and spends many happy evenings and weekends painting scenery, collecting stage props, and learning lines for the next play to be produced. Her growth is off the job; and, while her work may not suffer as a result of her outside interests, there may easily be fewer innovations in secretarial practices and a general emphasis on retaining "status quo" in the office.

Harold Oldfield is a shop worker. At one time he had hoped to become a foreman; but, as he finds his boss reacting negatively to every suggestion made by an employee, hears him talk as though the superintendent were one of the world's most unreasonable men, and sees him struggling—with constant complaints—to handle all the required paperwork, he begins to find the 3:30 P.M. quitting time "without a worry in the world" a wonderful thing. It gives him time to spend with his young children, and "what is more important for a father anyway?" And so his values and interests become focused almost solely on his home and his family.

Is it right that John should find his development in his job and wrong that Mary and Harold should find it in other parts of their lives? No. The issue is not one of wrong or right. It is that growth and development will occur regardless of whatever steps the manager takes. To insure that some of it occurs on the job is the manager's responsibility. To point out the directions in which development is needed—and may be well rewarded in terms of fuller use of one's talents or in terms of company recognition or career advancement— is a much neglected opportunity. To provide conditions in which such growth appears attractive and successful efforts to grow are recognized is neither expensive nor time consuming. Both require example, attention, and some acquired skill on the part of managers.

A manager should engage in some self-brainwashing and put aside the notion that development means something extra, something dissociated from assigned work. Instead, he should think of development as increased capacity for getting results. He should recognize, of course, that a given employee may wish to grow, or may have a greater capacity to grow, along other lines than are suggested by the man's present work or job. He should also recognize, however, that as a manager he has a responsibility to both the employee and the firm to promote the opportunities for development at least in the employee's current job and to provide conditions that will encourage the employee to take steps in the desired developmental direction.

Don't Managers Already Do This?

In these terms it somehow seems both too easy and too hard. Easy because, after all, isn't this pretty much what most managers already do? They delegate or assign work and then, by pointing out where the employee is and is not meeting managerial standards, they let him see where improvement—development—is needed. And, if they supply reasonably adequate physical surroundings and the tools and equipment needed to do the work, there is no reason why the desired improvement should not be achieved. But, in contrast, delegating work which requires the employee to acquire new knowledge and skills may involve a truly creative effort on the manager's part. Moreover, making it attractive for the employee to strive for development rather than feel like a small child taken to task for

failing to do all his father expects may be one of the
more complex managerial skills.

This brings us to the last two basic concepts to be
discussed here: Work, to be developmental, should
require the employee to learn and apply new knowledge and skills. And, for best results, the manager
should be sure the employee sees the development
effort as serving his personal interest as well as those of
the firm.

The young engineer, John Jones, had work to do
which by its very nature required him to add to his
technical competence. Provided he had the necessary
talent and his manager did not deliberately, if unconsciously, make it undesirable for him to learn, technical
development at least was almost certain to result.

But not all jobs have this high level of innovation.
What of Mary Smith and her secretarial position? To
work with Mary to evolve some new areas for achievement without sacrificing the already high volume of her
day-to-day activity requires interest, attention, and some
creative thinking on both sides. And to do it in such a
way that Mary sees it as an attractive proposition rather
than a deliberate attempt to add unwanted, unneeded
burdens to her full day implies a high level of communication based on a relationship between Mary and her
manager that would have to be built carefully over a
long period of time. Perhaps Mary's boss might show his
concern that her job is becoming dull, routine. Together
they might determine where major portions of her time
are going and set themselves the goal of finding an
easier, less time-consuming way of getting some of the
chores done, so that Mary can handle, say, a share of the
charting work. The search for a better way of coping
with the correspondence and other routine tasks, plus
the additional charting, should provide new job elements

calling for Mary's further development. But they are likely to be successful only if Mary sees them as adding to her importance and taking her in the direction of her own interests. So Mary's boss needs to explore rather carefully with her what these interests are; he needs to be prepared to describe alternatives in case Mary doesn't really know where she would like her career to take her. Then, once he has encouraged her to begin improvement efforts, he needs to display sustained interest and encouragement so that Mary feels her effort is recognized.

Harold's interest in becoming a foreman could have been sustained, too, though not with his foreman continuing to make it appear an unattractive job. Now Harold will have to seek other ways of learning what a foreman's job can be like and how he might master various parts of it for which he has no training. Unfortunately, it doesn't appear probable that he will be motivated to do this. The development action in this case must begin a level higher—between the foreman and his boss.

How the Manager Achieves
Employee Development Goals

Once the manager grasps the fundamental concepts, he should next understand exactly what work is required of him if he is to achieve his employee development goals. Just as in the case of all other managerial responsibilities, he should (1) take the lead in providing sound information so that the employee sees clearly the opportunity for personal development in work useful to the organization; (2) help the employee to set sound development goals; (3) provide opportunities for the employee to reach his goals; and (4) establish the climate which makes effort toward these goals attractive.

Development information. The manager has two sources of information that usually are not available to the employee except through him. He should have knowledge of business plans and strategy both for his own organization and for components above him which should provide a basis for seeing where major job opportunities are likely to occur. He should also have information about the company's manpower plans which tells him the kinds and numbers of technological and managerial skills which will be needed overall and which, in effect, indicate the sort of development he is expected to accomplish for the company.

Whether or not the manager is a good appraiser of employee potential, and whether or not he understands the employee's career goals and desires for improvement or advancement, he should be able to discuss these opportunities intelligently. If the employee is aware of what is being planned for the future, he can think about himself in this context and make choices based on his own feelings and interests. The information needs, of course, to be current so that as ideas evolve and situations change, the employee can adapt accordingly.

And, remember, quite apart from future opportunity there is the essential question of positive improvement in handling current responsibilities. While the employee may be better at seeing how his performance falls short *now* than he is at visualizing future opportunities, here, too, the manager has a contribution to offer. His perspective on organization needs as a whole and his more objective view of the employee's contribution to them make it important for him to share his thoughts and ideas.

Development goals. Information is useful but not enough, in itself, to insure development. This is likely to occur only if employee and manager alike are committed to certain goals which are clearly specified. There are two issues here. The first is to be sure that the goals are sound and well conceived. The second is to be sure that they are fully accepted by both employee and manager.

Sound, well-conceived goals are goals which serve the interests of both the business and the employee. They have as their source an understanding of the work, current and anticipated, which the firm needs; the environment or the conditions in which it is needed; and the employee's talents and interests. The match is unlikely to be perfect; but, since needs, environment, and even employee capabilities all are constantly changing and dynamic, a reasonable match is usually possible.

To insure the manager's commitment, any development goal must be relevant to his personal responsibilities. This, in effect, means his manager must not only support the goal but also make work demands on him which can be met only if the goal is accomplished. Real success will be most likely if the goal relates to plans for current work improvement or manpower development which come from a higher level in the organization. Ideally, of course, the manager should have had a chance to take part in evolving these goals and plans.

Obtaining the employee's commitment may be harder. Again, if he proposes it for himself on the basis of information received from the manager, or if he is sufficiently involved in setting it that he feels a stake in its achievement, his commitment is probable. Admiration and respect for the manager and the feeling that his best interests are being considered may also lead to ready acceptance, as may a strong attachment to the organization. The loyal employee who sees certain work accomplishments as necessary to the firm's success will probably try to meet those goals, even knowing he must upgrade both knowledge and skill. And, of course, the man who sees a particular accomplishment as advancing his personal career desires will usually do his best to make it a reality.

All these conditions reflect an attitude on the employee's part which the manager must earn. They are, however, no different from the attitudes that must be earned in order to accomplish any work goals successfully.

Development opportunity. Nothing is so likely to hamper accomplishment as agreeing to work toward specified development goals and then discovering that needed resources are not available, that time is so scarce and priority so low that almost all other goals take precedence. Goals should be set only if the manager can provide the opportunity for achieving them. Take Manager X and the employee whose product-testing program is off schedule. If, together, they set as the employee's goal the improvement of planning skills and improved relationships with purchasing, and Manager X then insists on stepping up the testing program so that the employee must spend 60 hours a week on it for the foreseeable future, planning skills probably won't improve to any extent. If Manager X sees a way in which planning can be improved during the testing, he needs to work with the employee, help him see how this can be done. And, in reviewing the results of the testing program, he must also look at possible improvement in the planning if he is serious about developing this skill.

Development climate. Given sound goals, commitment, and opportunity for achievement, the manager is responsible, further, for establishing the kind of climate that will sustain the employee's efforts toward accomplishment. The sort of atmosphere he creates will, of course, be a function of his style of managing; the long-term relationships existing among him, the employee, and other members of the organization; and all the other factors which normally affect the working habits of a component—the manager's personal attention, the form that attention takes, attention from the manager's manager, and so on.

Manager Y, for example, is trying to show the company's purchasing agent how much benefit would be gained by streamlining the paperwork system on competitive bidding. He feels that the very process would bring about real growth in the employee's understanding of the production system, increase his contacts with other members of the organization, and help improve his persuasive skills in certain important ways. Manager Y may believe the major battle is won when the employee is enthusiastic about undertaking the work. This particular purchasing agent, however, doesn't know where to begin; after a few days there is no visible action. In his effort to get the man "off the dime," Manager Y berates the purchasing agent sarcastically in front of his associates for his lack of initiative. Now, since the paperwork study represented a development area for the employee in the first place, presumably it was not the kind of project he was well equipped to tackle. Unfortunately, the climate created by Manager Y makes it unlikely that this purchasing agent will, in the future, be quite so enthusiastic about tackling new and unfamiliar jobs.

The climate factor is not really as nebulous as the word sometimes seems. It is primarily a matter of the emphasis or priority the manager places on development effort. And it depends almost wholly on the encouragement he gives the individual employee, even when the results are not as satisfactory as he might wish, and the positive recognition with which he rewards success.

Favorable Interaction = Development

From this discussion it is clear that three factors are continuously involved in the development process:

1. The employee himself—his abilities, his knowledge and skill, his attitudes, his interests and values, his career aspirations.
2. The work for which the employee is responsible or which is asked of him—its demands for new knowledge and skill or for changes in attitudes, interests, or values.
3. The climate, situation, or environment in which the work is undertaken and carried out—including the manager's style of managing, his attitudes and interests, the pressures on the organization, the facilities available, the incentives for development, and all the other tangible and intangible elements which make action easy or hard.

It is the favorable interaction of these three which produces development in the occupational sense. And, of the three, it is the manager who exerts the most influence. He selects the employee, assigns the work, and evaluates the man's success at it. He is perhaps the key element in the prevailing climate, and he is certainly in a position to "make or break" the employee so far as his future in the organization is concerned. Therefore, it is natural that the major burden for development should be his responsibility.

To do the work of development—gathering and communicating the necessary information for sound goal setting, providing opportunity to achieve tough goals, and making it attractive to do so—requires the manager to assess or appraise each of these three factors as they are now, evolve targets for their change, and, finally, carry out specific action plans to bring about the desired results.

CHAPTER III

FOCUSING DEVELOPMENT GOALS
ON WORK COMMITMENTS

DEVELOPMENT FOR WHAT? A MANAGER WHO FACES HIS development responsibilities realistically is confronted with two major considerations. These have been stated earlier, but they bear repeating: Employee development will most likely have useful, productive results for the firm if the direction of planned growth contributes in a substantial way to current or anticipated business needs. The employee, however, will probably participate wholeheartedly only if he sees the effort as contributing to his personal interests, leading him in the direction of his career goals.

Step 1 for the manager, then, involves systematic identification of a variety of development targets serving the mutual advantage of the firm and the employee. He needs to be objective and realistic about these targets. At the same time he needs to avoid unwanted invasion of the employee's personal life and unwarranted meddling with the employee's career. He should not be too general, for a general growth target—to become a better or more productive worker, for example—seldom has a marked impact on employee effectiveness. It is hard to plan, even harder to implement, and almost impossible to measure. The more specific the development targets, therefore, the more likely the employee is to achieve them and the more likely he is to realize that he has achieved them. The resulting sense of success provides impetus for setting new development targets so that the whole process is reinforced and often accelerated.

The most logical source for such specific goals is the work the employee is doing currently or might logically be doing within a reasonably short time. This is because both employee and manager are already committed to certain work accomplishments and improvement of their joint ability to achieve them. And, regardless of what overall development plans exist in a firm, an improved contribution to the total effort is almost certain to be required of everyone.

There are, however, dangers connected with work targets. It is easy to set goals which represent sheer improvement in employee efficiency or output, if only because people are working longer hours. These do indicate, it is true, some change in a person's capabilities or values, but they do not represent the acquisition of those powerful new skills or that greater commitment to innovative accomplishment which is the kind of growth usually needed from professional, supervisory, and managerial employees.

Another danger is that the development goal may be imposed on what already appears to be a full workload. The manager who sets work goals should be prepared for early investment of some working time—with confidence that later payoff will justify it. The company's objectives and philosophy of development, of course, help the individual manager determine what investment is warranted at any particular time. But the fact of the current time sacrifice makes it even more imperative that the goal to be achieved have real potential for increasing the value of the employee's contribution.

Then, too, a manager may select development goals without adequate consultation with his manager and associates. It is for this reason that development goals should be handled like other managerial work—that agreement about them should be reached between supervisors and managers at successive levels in the organization. This helps insure coordination toward meaningful overall results and support, measurement, and recognition from above.

Targets in Current Company Needs

One method of choosing sound employee development goals is to compare the work that is needed with the current performance capability of the employee. Proper comparison implies an accurate appraisal of both these factors. How does a manager make such appraisals? What management tools are available to help him? The word "tools" may seem strange since available instruments bear little resemblance to the sophisticated tools of the physical scientist. They are, however, information-producing devices which help a manager make needed judgmental decisions. Fortunately, in the current work and performance area most companies offer a number of useful ones. Among them are the job description and work plan (as sources of future needed work targets) and the work history or résumé, performance appraisal, and work sampling (for acquiring information on the status of current capability). Let's look at each of these in turn.

Job description. A job or position description is a written summary of the major responsibilities to be handled by the incumbent of a given position. It usually includes a statement of the purpose of the position (the reason why the job is needed); a list of key duties, with some indication of how their successful performance will be measured; and any specific ways in which the authority of the incumbent is limited—for example, in spending money or signing contracts. Some of the more sophisticated job descriptions may also include major working relationships with other members of the firm. Since this is somewhat rare, the description usually needs to be read with the organization in mind so that the job is viewed within the context of related positions. (See Suggested Form 1 for sample items from a typical job description.)

To identify development targets, the manager reads the job description and, from the list of duties or responsibilities and the relationships stated or implied, earmarks those which in his judgment are most important to the success of the department and to which he feels the employee needs to give greater emphasis.

Work plan. Occasionally, job descriptions are out of date or written in such general terms that they do not lend themselves well to identifying future work targets. A currently popular alternative is the work plan. This is an outline of specific pieces of work to be accomplished by the employee during the next three months to one year. It translates the business needs of the total organization into terms of the individual's contribution to them. It consists of goals which define the results the employee is to achieve, a series of major actions to be taken to reach each goal, a timetable for each, and the measures to be used to determine success. It may also include a statement of resources needed; that is, manpower, money, tools, equipment, and so on. (See Suggested Form 2 for sample items.)

SUGGESTED FORM 1

JOB DESCRIPTION: SAMPLE ITEMS

Title of Position: Engineering Administration Specialist
Reports to: Manager of Engineering
   Electronic Control Department

Purpose of Position: To provide the Manager of Engineering with basic information about (1) the capabilities and resources of the engineering department for the purpose of proposing and negotiating work contracts and (2) status of contracts already accepted. To provide specified pooled personnel services for the department.

Specific Responsibilities and Their Measurement:

1. Maintain accurate statistical data on numbers, educational preparation, specialized skills, and similar information about current employees of the department. Measured by: accuracy and availability of data needed for customer proposals, company manpower and facility reports, and operation of a promotion system for technical employees.

2. Operate a critical path method of work control (such as PERT) so as to highlight areas of work progress and anticipated deficiencies in accomplishment. Measured by: manager's estimate of use-

fulness in directing attention toward needed areas; satisfaction of government requirements for defense projects.

3. Negotiate contract terms, including pricing arrangements, with customers after the decision has been made to undertake the work. Measured by: manager's judgment of adequacy of final terms.

4. Recruit engineers, scientists, and technicians as required by department commitments. . . . Measured by: planned personnel available and qualified.

Important Relationships: Obtain data on oral and written basis for record-keeping and programming functions. Provide service to all managers of the department on pooled personnel services. Advise key managers on matters of budget, cost estimating, time estimating, and similar items in connection with contract negotiation and administration functions. Provide a coordinating function with respect to these inputs. . . .

Reserved Authority: Maximum expenditure authorized: $20,000. Authorized to sign contracts committing the company up to $150,000 maximum. Personnel actions: hiring, firing, promotions, and compensation, subject to approval of Manager of Engineering. . . .

Step 1: **Manager circles "hot" items for next year which might represent employee development targets.**

SUGGESTED FORM 2

WORK PLAN: SAMPLE ITEMS

Position: Engineering Administration Specialist
Period of Time: January 1-June 30

Goal 1. Update information in manpower inventory by March 1.

Task 1. Review questionnaire used in past and revise so as to eliminate information no longer used; simplify completion of form and its coding for keypunch operation. January 16.

Task 2. Develop a schedule for each organization in the department to update for its personnel. January 21.

Task 3. Launch a persuasive employee communication program to encourage employee cooperation in this much disliked task. February 1.

Task 4. Implement the schedule in Task 2, providing weekly feedback to employees and managers on extent to which task has been completed. February 4-May 1.

Task 5. Check completed forms on a 20% sample basis. February 4-May 1.

Task 6. Work with coding and keypunch operators for their understanding and help devise ways of improving accuracy of their function. . . .

Requires approximately one hour of each employee's time to complete questionnaire; requires 200 hours coding and keypunch time and 3 hours data processing time. . . .

Alternate or Additional Step 1: Manager circles a goal important to next year's work or susceptible to a different approach, sets an earlier date, or picks a knowledge or skill area which supports goal or task accomplishment. For example: Revise Tasks 1 and 6 so that each technical employee codes his own information. Or: Learn fundamentals of business programming.

There are at least two options for the manager who uses work plans as a source of employee development targets. He can read through the plan and identify one or more goals which are to be given more emphasis, which might be reached by a different course of action than the one planned (one that would provide business benefits and also challenge the employee's abilities), or which might be reached sooner than planned, giving both a competitive advantage and an opportunity for the employee to increase certain capabilities. Or he can add to the work plan a specific growth goal for which the employee must then develop a plan. This might include improvement in on-going or recurring work elements, such as a system or process, or it might specify a needed increase in a particular knowledge or skill.

Information on Current Employee Performance

From either job description or work plan, or both, the manager compiles a short list of work or skill areas in which the employee might improve and so make a greater contribution to meeting company needs. Before deciding whether some or all represent high-priority development goals for this employee, he must factor in sound judgments of the employee's current work capabilities. Data for the purpose should be readily available in such forms as the employee's work history or résumé, recent performance appraisals, or work sampling. How does each of these provide needed information?

Work history or résumé. A look at what the employee's past jobs have been and what experiences he has had may yield some strengths on which to capitalize and some gaps to be filled in. Granted, the typical writ-

SUGGESTED FORM 3

PERFORMANCE APPRAISAL SUMMARY: SAMPLE ITEMS

Position: Engineering Administration Specialist
Period of Time: January 1-June 30

Major Contributions:

1. Collected current manpower inventory information on 93% of the department's technical personnel. Improved method of collection and recording to save time of professional employees.

2. Negotiated incentive contract with ABC Bureau which provides opportunity for upgrading profit on this kind of business. This was done in spite of a trend in the reverse direction.

3. In a very tight engineering manpower market, recruited 62 engineers and scientists, thus meeting departmental needs.

Development Opportunities:

1. Improved knowledge of data preparation and processing would help both in operation of critical path planning and in maximizing use of manpower and other inventories.

2. Relationships with associates would be more effective if he understood the total picture of paperwork demands on their time more fully and could thus do a better overall scheduling job with respect to his requests of them. . . .

Step 2: Manager earmarks performance strength on which to build or improvement opportunity. Examples from above: Fuller use of manpower inventory in customer proposals and better understanding of line manager's total paperwork.

ten work history in the form of a résumé may not be too useful for this purpose, but an employee interview to supplement the basic information may be very helpful.

Performance appraisal. While managers necessarily appraise the performance of those who report to them on a frequent if not a continuing basis throughout the year, this is usually an informal, mental appraisal. Most companies, however, ask the manager to state in writing his opinion of the employee's performance on the job and call the result "the performance appraisal."[1] It is most successful when it is based on responsibilities listed in the job description or in the work plan against which the employee has been working. In this way it documents work accomplishments and failures. In addition, it should call attention to any conditions existing during the appraisal period which made it easier or harder for the employee to accomplish his work. (See Suggested Form 3 for sample items.)

If performance appraisals are made and recorded every year, the manager has a further advantage in that he is able to go back in time and note changes or trends in the employee's capabilities. He can log significant strengths on which the employee might build and areas of ignorance or inexperience, *related to important work ahead,* which are within his ability to change.

Usually a performance appraisal is thought of as a document, prepared by the supervisor or manager, which concerns the employee's work. In favor at various times during the past quarter-century is the employee *self-appraisal,* highly praised by certain managers who find it works well for them. Essentially this is a document, usually in the prescribed performance appraisal form, which is prepared by the employee for discussion

[1] See Kellogg, Marion S., *What to Do About Performance Appraisal,* American Management Association, 1965.

SUGGESTED FORM 4

Employee's Accomplishment Inventory:
Sample Items

Position: Engineering Administration Specialist
Period of Time: January 1-June 30

1. Reviewed and streamlined form for data collection of employee qualifications. Accuracy of stored information increased greatly by developing simple self-coding system whereby employee did his own coding and keypunch operation was merely copied. Completed inventory updating on schedule.

2. Recruited two outstanding senior electronic systems specialists: J. H. Hart and N. O. Pauling.

3. In spite of great opposition from contracting agency, devised an incentive contract plan and won acceptance. This gives us the chance to improve our profit picture by as much as 5% on this contract. . . .

Alternate or Additional Step 2: Manager earmarks performance strength or area for improvement. Examples from above: Needs better picture of department's paperwork system. Talent for price negotiation should be exploited.

with his manager and which represents his opinion of his work insofar as he is willing to state it for the record.

In a self-appraisal situation, the employee completes the form and presents it to his manager. The manager reinforces the points on which they are in agreement, and the two discuss the points of disagreement till they reach a consensus or at least understand the reasons for their differences.

Self-appraisal is a sound tool provided the manager has done his homework. What was expected of the employee must have been clearly understood between them, and the manager's standards for judging success or degrees of success must also have been communicated and agreed to. The channels of information exchange must have been open throughout the appraisal period so that the employee has had good feedback on the manager's reaction to his work, behavior, and methods.

A variation of the self-appraisal is the so-called *joint appraisal*. Both manager and employee complete the form, and it is discussed in much the same way as the self-appraisal. Either technique is useful in attempting to formulate development goals because the areas indicated as needing improvement not only represent opportunities for development but have the added advantage of almost certain employee acceptance since they result from his own analysis of his work.

In the *accomplishment inventory*, still another version of self-appraisal, the employee is asked to document on, say, an annual basis the key contributions he believes he has made to the business. He describes them in detail, giving as much information about circumstances that made them easy or hard as he feels necessary. (See Suggested Form 4.) Although such a statement naturally is biased, it is extremely useful as a record of work if annotated by the manager and discussed to the point where each man understands the other's view of specific items. Thus it, too, provides a basis for managerial assessment of the employee's current work capability.

Work sampling. Some of the information obtained from performance appraisals may be contradictory or confusing, especially when prepared by different managers who have different standards and values or when manager and employee evaluations are being compared. For this reason it is well to supplement written appraisal information with some current firsthand work sampling.

The term "work sampling" is more frequently used in connection with hourly jobs or jobs which are repetitive in nature. In factory situations, "job analysis," "job audit," "time and motion study," and the like are all work sampling methods. A trained observer watches the employee at work and records in more or less elaborate detail what he does, how he does it, and how long it takes. These data, accumulated during one or preferably several typical work periods, are then compared with standards which have been built statistically by observation of other employees doing similar work or performing similar actions.

In more complex positions, attempts have been made from time to time[2] to keep track of what is done: meetings held, people contacted, length of time involved, and so on. But, since there are no general standards to use for comparative purposes, work sampling has proved primarily useful as an exploratory device or one for improving the management of one's own time.

There is every reason, however, for a manager to do a little work sampling of his own on an informal basis.

[2] See, for example, Carlson, Sune, *Executive Behavior,* C. A. Strömberg Aktiebolag, Stockholm, Sweden, 1951.

It is especially appropriate in situations where an employee is new, where work has changed substantially, or where documented appraisal data are incomplete or contradictory. The manager simply determines the kind of at-work situation in which he wants to see the employee—defending his budget proposal or handling a large meeting, for example. He finds out when a situation of this kind is scheduled, then goes and listens. In fact, he selects several such situations, if possible, and decides in advance what it is that he wants to know about the employee in those circumstances. Thus his observations can be as specific as possible.

Work sampling need not, of course, be an active situation in which the employee is observed *doing* something. It may equally well be a study of his actual output as typified by a piece of mathematical analysis he has done, a breadboard design, or something as simple as file copies of a stenographer's typing. The point is that a manager requires factual evidence from a real work situation if he is to make an accurate, up-to-date appraisal for development purposes. And his judgment will be useful only insofar as the sampling is related to things the employee will need to know and do *in the work ahead.*

Work sampling has its variations too. Methods, processes, and systems studies are versions of the technique with emphasis on the flow of work between organizations, between individuals in an organization, or both. The observer or individual charged with the study documents the way in which the work moves from one individual to another and what happens to it at each stage. This is particularly valuable in reviewing paperwork systems which are suspected of being too burdensome and needing streamlining or mechanization. With the help of charting techniques and flow diagrams, the

course of the work is pictured so that the steps can be
defined and the work at each simplified without loss of
any essential element. Changes in work processes or systems often require individuals to change what they do
and develop new skills, becoming broader and more
flexible or, possibly, more specialized. Thus they are a
good source of specific, short-term development goals.

Growth Targets in Longer-Range Business Plans

From a comparison of opportunities for work payoff
now and in the future against the employee's current
performance strengths and areas of ignorance or inexperience, the manager is able to identify a number of
sound development goals. But there is a second cluster
of comparisons which also yields sound development
goals. It is concerned with the longer-range direction of
the growth of the business as compared with its current
status and trends.

Almost every company has some longer-range plans
for the future. These plans may be based on market
research data, anticipated technological or product
development, financial considerations, knowledge of
competitors' moves, and so on. For larger businesses
they are in writing and include basic strategies as well
as the rough timing of major events and the financial
investment required. In small companies they may be in
discussion form only, evolved at meetings of the firm's
top management and the board of directors.

The manager seeking sound growth targets for
employees familiarizes himself with at least the general
nature of such plans and reaches agreement with his
manager as to how the anticipated changes are likely to
affect the individuals in his organization. On the basis

of this information he identifies several areas in which his organization will need new skills or knowledge. These become development targets for appropriate employees at appropriate points in time. For example, the factory superintendent in a company primarily active in the defense industry may learn that volume production is expected to fall off during the next five years and custom work increase. Aside from the implications for the numbers of people needed, there may well be questions of shop rearrangement to consider, perhaps less specialization by individual workers and greater emphasis on quality of product. All these provide important development targets for different employees. And they are needed soon enough to permit rapid application of whatever new capabilities are acquired.

Manpower planning. The formal translation of business plans into the people required, taking into consideration such factors as normal turnover, mobility, and retirement, is called manpower planning. It does not usually go so far as to define individual jobs to be filled except at the very top of the company, but it provides data on the numbers of managers, the numbers and types of technologically skilled professionals, and the numbers of personnel in various other categories that will be needed.

A manager looking over such data can see what talents are most likely to be in demand within a certain time period and select appropriate targets for given individuals. He should not, obviously, take the firm's manpower plan and try to apply it to his organization independently. If all the managers in the company were to do this, duplication and gaps would inevitably result. To be effective, the use of the manpower plan as a source of development targets needs to be spearheaded

SUGGESTED FORM 5

SAMPLE RUNNER-UP CHART

Manager—Engineering John Q. Altman		
Henry R. Tobler	Age	Color Code
John L. Noble	Age	Color Code
Roy C. Houser	Age	Color Code

Manager—XYZ Project Henry R. Tobler		
John L. Noble	Age	Color Code
Peter C. Daniels	Age	Color Code
Carl D. King	Age	Code Color

Manager—Design Engineering Roy C. Houser		
Peter C. Daniels	Age	Color Code
Lester Morris	Age	Color Code
Daniel L. Prince	Age	Color Code

Code: Green: ready now
Blue: ready in one or two years
Red: ready in three to five years
White: not likely to be qualified, but
best available

Alternate or Additional Step 1: Manager identifies what H. R. Tobler should learn to do in order to qualify for Manager-Engineering; what P. C. Daniels needs for either Project Manager or Design Engineering Manager; and so on for all the individuals involved.

and integrated from the top of the organization component or company so that the managers will be working as a team.

Runner-up charts. A manager draws up a chart of his
organization as it will probably be at some specified
point in the future. Beneath the name of each likely
incumbent, including his own, he lists the names of
currently and potentially qualified successors. Usually
he is asked to limit the runners-up to three and to indicate by some code how well qualified each man is to
succeed to the job or how soon he will be ready to take
on the responsibilities of the job. (See Suggested Form 5
for an example.)

If an employee is listed as a runner-up for one or
more jobs, the manager reviews the probable major
requirements of the jobs to identify those which the
employee does not yet meet but which the manager
feels are within his capability. These requirements
represent possible development targets. For example,
if a position involves a large number of employees and
the employee's experience has so far been limited to
working with small groups, such skills as communication
within large groups and planning involving several
organization levels might be excellent goals for individual growth.

The use of the runner-up chart in this way is quite
profitable, especially if a manager selects, insofar as possible, requirements which are likely to be common to
many jobs and avoids telling the employee that he is a
runner-up for any specific one. Instead, he might be
told that his good work is recognized and that there
probably will be a number of opportunities requiring
such and such a skill or such and such experience.
Whenever it is economically reasonable to do so, the
manager should build the needed skill or experience

into the framework of the present job so that the emphasis remains on current contribution and does not shift to speculation about advancement.

Clues to Company Progress Toward Goals

The manager has now succeeded in identifying growth targets through his study of the company's plans for the future and through a process of matching probable opportunities with his best estimate of his employees' abilities. But he must check from time to time to see what progress the company is making against its plans and whether the expected opportunities are likely to arrive on schedule. There are a number of methods he can use.

Analysis of business results. Almost all managers receive information on current business results at frequent intervals. It takes the form of figures on actual expenditures against budget, product performance against specifications, manpower against budget, product quality, shipments against schedule, waste and spoilage, rework, down time, sales billed, backlog of orders, customer complaints—all the rest. Such data provide a very specific and practical appraisal of the organization's position. Fluctuations and trends indicate, to those with sufficient experience to interpret them, the direction in which things are moving. By noting these trends, and using them as a basis for comparison with long-range plans, managers can identify critical discrepancies and so verify development goals.

Manpower inventory. A manpower inventory is a listing of some or all of the organization's employees together with their education, their skills and experience, and such other important personal data as retirement date and physical limitations, if any, which may rule out certain kinds of work. It is essentially an attempt to assess the manpower on hand so that recruiting and training can be synchronized with anticipated needs. Advanced data processing systems have made such inventories more readily available in recent years.

The individual manager can use inventory data to pinpoint needs which many employees may be expected to share, but he will then have to judge whether a particular need represents a desirable development goal for a given employee. For example, even if manpower plans indicate that 35 managers will be required for a new plant and the manpower inventory shows 20 on hand, the manager must still decide whether Tom Smith should begin learning managing skills. And presumably Tom will have some say in the decision too.

Estimates of Employee Potential and Growth Rates

In his attempts to look into the future, the manager also is forced to predict the likely direction and rate of an employee's growth if he is to select meaningful development goals. The basis for making such predictions is very shaky indeed. Thoughtful review of performance appraisals made over several years' time may indicate areas of performance capability that have been growing, others that have leveled off. Gaps in experience may become obvious.

In a later chapter, some of the more advanced techniques for making judgments about employee potential will be discussed. In general, however, trends in performance as observed or documented in appraisal records, plus clues from interests and abilities displayed either on or off the job, provide the best available source of information for the manager. These, viewed in the light of long-range plans for the growth of the business, are fundamental to selecting sound individual goals.

All the target-setting tools we have described are attempts to predict in a formal way what is likely to happen to the company—or what management would like to have happen—at some point in the future and how the individual is likely to fit into this changed picture. They alert both manager and employee to needed knowledge and skills sufficiently in advance that a person can make real progress in selected areas and be "waiting in the wings." Moreover, since he is aware of the direction the business is taking, the employee feels he is "in on things" and is an important part of the organization.

Often, however, long-range plans fail to materialize as expected. Or their timing is off and both employee

Tools for Setting Work-Based Development Goals

	Target Setting	Status Appraisal

Current Work	Job Description
	Work Plan
		Work History, Résumé
		Performance Appraisal
		Self-Appraisal, Joint
		  Appraisal, Accomplishment
		  Inventory
		Work Sampling
		  Job Analysis
		  Time and Motion Study
		  Measured Time Sampling
		  Methods, Processes, or
		  Systems Study

Future Work	Longer-Range Business Plans Manpower Plans Runner-up Charts	Business Results Data Manpower Inventory Appraisal of Potential

and manager find themselves ready with knowledge and skills long before these are needed—or, indeed, ready for an eventuality that never comes to pass. Knowledge may have to be refreshed and skills relearned, thus penalizing the first learning effort. Frustration and discouragement may result.

Since, therefore, greater risks are incurred in deriving development targets from future plans than in relying on current work, the manager should discuss matters with the employee pretty frankly. Insofar as possible, he should share with the employee the information on which he is basing his recommendations. In this way, the employee participates in the goal-setting decision and is less likely to feel bitter if the company's plans do not work out. The development goals chosen should preferably be drawn from the earlier stages of plans, and they should represent growth in types of skill or knowledge which might have more than one application. And they should be reconsidered at frequent intervals in the light of new developments so that changes from the original business plans can be spotted early and incorporated into revised growth plans as soon as possible. If it seems clear that the employee's talents are not suited to the future course of the business, the manager should probably restrict his recommendations to development goals based on the employee's current work or on some currently needed talent or ability the employee possesses but has not yet been able to display. Developing this sort of latent capacity is particularly appropriate if it will provide the employee with an alternate path for career growth.

There is no question that adequate *means* of identifying goals are available. The manager's problem may well be one of choosing among them before attempting to choose among the possible goals. In the case of nonexempt employees, factory workers, and office workers, the job description—along with some work sampling and an accurate performance appraisal—is usually both practical and sound. For technicians, professionals, and supervisors or managers, work and business plans plus a self-appraisal/work sampling combination make a more likely choice.

On the whole, work-based goals represent the least risk, the best promise for growth, no matter what the category of employee. Not only do they mean the least sacrifice of current results, but they may well bring the greatest improvement in current results. That is why every manager should establish at least one work-based development goal for each employee reporting to him.

CHAPTER IV

FACTORING CLIMATE INTO
DEVELOPMENT GOALS

No MAN WORKS IN A VACUUM. EACH IS SURROUNDED BY situational factors which help or hinder his productive output. In earlier days, working conditions were largely thought of as physical: heat, ventilation, lighting, noise level. In modern times, physical surroundings are usually excellent; so attention has shifted to more sophisticated factors. These may include the organization structure within which the employee functions, the resources available to him, the schedules he must meet, the information that is regularly at his disposal, the managing style of his own manager, and even broader influences from the company, the economy, and the socio-political system of which the business is a part.

Most managers concede the importance of such factors when they try to fill an open job with a man who will "fit in." Certainly, most recognize at least unconsciously the effect of environment, atmosphere, climate —whatever they may call it—on work output when they reorganize to meet commitments, set higher standards to improve quality, or introduce competitive contests to increase production. Few, however, take advantage of the full opportunity to use climate (the fashionable term these days) to make development goals of employees more incisive—that is, more directly conducive to increased contribution and individual career advancement.

The Key Climate Factors Considered

Let's look at each of the key climate factors to understand better how it can sharpen the focus of employee development goals.

Organization structure. Usually, organization is depicted by a chart which shows the vertical reporting relationships among positions in a company or component. It gives the title of each position with the name of the current incumbent. If titles have been well chosen, they reflect the incumbent's major responsibilities.

There are at least three ways in which a manager uses organization structure to strengthen employee development goals. First, he considers the working relationships a given employee has with other members of the firm (including himself). Then, basing his decision on payoff to the business, he selects one or two of these relationship areas where he feels the employee needs improvement to get better results. He doesn't urge the employee to make good resolutions like "Improve relationships with the field sales force"; rather, he links the development goal to a specific work goal. For example: "In order to improve sales of the new *ABC* product, increase face-to-face information sessions with the field sales force, including product demonstration, better descriptive literature, and more inputs on *ABC*'s superiority over the competitor's product." This tells the employee what is to be accomplished by the improved relationship, and the goal's specific content makes it more likely to be achieved.

A second way is to identify an area of the organization which does not seem to be functioning as efficiently as it should and assign this as a special study to a given employee (or a group of employees). The development goal is to learn about the work in this area and the problems hampering it so as to devise and recommend an effective organization change. The employee benefits, of course, both from familiarizing himself with the work in the problem area and from his increased knowledge of how to organize. But an important additional opportunity is implicit in this situation. The development goals of all the employees whose responsibilities or working relationships are affected by the recommended changes should be restructured correspondingly.

The third possibility for the manager is that offered by a major reorganization which alters the overall flow of work in significant ways and thus changes basic working relationships. Every business faces such major upheavals from time to time. While they are designed specifically to improve business results and make it easier for the organization to meet its commitments, they also may lead to useful shifts in employee development goals. Managers at all levels, beset with the inevitable problems accompanying reorganization, will naturally want to smooth the transition period. Therefore, each will work carefully with every employee reporting to him in order to set work goals which will utilize for development purposes the new organization structure within which they must be attained. For example, if product appearance design has been a decentralized function and pooled service is introduced in order to give the product line a recognizable "family look," this family look should become a goal of the appearance design group. In addition, to emphasize the function's new service role, each employee's work goals should reflect the need for improved information exchange with engineers, packaging experts, advertising staff, sales personnel, and so on.

Resources. To do a given piece of work, an employee is allocated certain resources by his manager. These include the money budgeted for the job, the manpower (or, if only one employee is involved, the percentage of his time) assigned to it, and the space, facilities, tools, and other equipment available for use. Most managers periodically review such resources to be sure they are adequate, commensurate with the priority of the work, and used at a reasonable rate.

As a result of this review, a manager may decide that it would be desirable to allocate a different amount of money to the work, assign fewer or more personnel, or make changes in facilities or tools. His decision is necessarily determined by what is best from the standpoint of the work itself, but factored into it may be the development implications for the employee. If the amount of money available is reduced, will this represent an opportunity for the employee to learn to manage funds more effectively? If so, let's make improved money management a part of the employee's plans. If personnel are increased, will this represent an opportunity to improve certain supervisory skills? If so, let's have a goal in this area. If special equipment is provided, will this represent an opportunity for added know-how? Let's be specific.

But suppose there is no change at all in available resources. Can the employee's performance still warrant the establishment of an improvement goal in one or more resource areas? Absolutely. Even if, for example, the money allocated is about right the employee may be spending at too rapid a rate. In this case the manager can set him the goal of bringing spending in line with budget. This doesn't sound like a development goal? It will be if the manager asks that the employee's plans for meeting it include specific steps which will add to his knowledge of money management: counseling with others who have done well in this area, devising specific cost controls suited to his work, and the like.

Work schedules. A sequence of tasks to be followed by an employee or a group of employees from the beginning to the end of a task or project is called a schedule. It is a familiar management tool.

The pressure of time, in fact, represents an excellent development opportunity. The manager reviews an employee's work against his schedule. Then, considering both business needs and employee work habits, he decides to speed up the work, slow it down, or let the schedule stand as is.

This tool's major development possibilities are improvements in the employee's planning skills, greater effectiveness in his allocation of resources, and innovation or increased efficiency brought about by tight deadlines. In addition, therefore, to involving the employee in schedule changes so that he clearly understands the reasons for them, the manager should set quite specific development goals which will lead the employee in the desired direction. For example, "Devise an improved method of working with subcontractors so that required quality is obtained and rework is reduced by one-third" (provided this will cut time out of a procurement schedule). Or: "Reduce the number of steps in the process from point of product sale to warehouse shipment, thus cutting the cycle to an average of ten days."

If the schedule itself is sound but the employee is not meeting it, goals should obviously be formulated to correct the situation, and the employee should make plans to meet them. If the schedule is sound and the employee is meeting it comfortably, then the manager may deliberately alter dates in one or two work areas where he feels the employee might use his ingenuity to reduce process time to the benefit of the business.

Information. In every organization there is a flow of information from manager to employee, from employee to manager, and from employee to employee. This information flow is facilitated by such devices as staff meetings or roundtables, business and project reviews, oral and written reports, and, of course, the more informal telephone and personal contacts.

Opportunities for sharpening development goals are to be found in better use of available information on the job, enlargement of information so that better work decisions can be made, and improved transmission of information so that others may perform more effectively. Examples: "Get more complete market research data on Product Y so that advertising is keyed more closely to customer desires." "Develop information on precedents established for business practices relating to the ABC Law so that compliance can be reviewed and policy formulated for future guidance." "Keep the *DEF* Company customer fully informed, on a weekly basis, of action taken on his product complaint so that he will feel that the full resources of the organization are devoted to correcting the problem." Note that in each case, to insure the best chance of meeting the goal, the results to be achieved are specified. Information may add to the employee's knowledge, but it is the application of information that brings about performance improvement.

Managing style. The term "managing style" covers a variety of things a manager or supervisor does in the day-to-day operation of his department: how he delegates work to employees, how he follows up on what has been delegated, how he communicates, what standards he sets, what methods he endorses, the extent to which he encourages employees to undertake calculated risks, and his system of reward and recognition. Also included are the somewhat more intangible attitudes, values, and personal qualities he displays while managing.

The manager's style is, in fact, probably the most important factor in the context within which most employees work. Development goals can therefore be made more potent by explicit statement of the manager's standards or values or attitudes so that employee energy can be devoted to cooperating with them rather than trying to find out what they are. Of course, in order to stimulate growth and improved performance, a manager may deliberately change some aspects of his style, and these changes can be incorporated into development goals with good results. For instance, the manager can increase or decrease the frequency with which he reviews the employee's work, he can introduce or withdraw certain formal communications, or he can encourage more or less risk taking. Any such action, obviously, must be keyed to the employee's maturity, competence, and performance level.

Broader influences. The situational factors considered so far have been primarily internal to the firm or to the organization within the firm. But, just as no employee works in a vacuum, so no company or subdivision of a company works in isolation. The philosophy, policies, objectives, and strategy of the total enterprise strongly affect the functioning climate of all components. If the company is highly decentralized, a local manager has considerable freedom of choice in making decisions and establishing management practices which fit *his* business.

If the company is highly centralized, he may have firm requirements established for him with which he and his organization must comply.

Moreover, the company is probably associated with a particular business or industry whose traditions and practices affect its methods of operation. Certainly the requirements of customers and the moves of competitors have a serious impact on working climate. Nor can government attitudes and legislation, the state of the economy, the international scene, and the cultures of countries in which the company functions be discounted in considering the total work environment. These broader influences are most likely to affect the goals of the president or perhaps the manager of a particular business or department, who will then transmit any necessary changes in direction down the organization line. For example, if competition is moving ahead on the strength of an aggressive national advertising campaign, the objective of countering this advantage will appear in the manager's own plans and, subsequently, in those of appropriate employees. Managing style may take on a sudden sense of urgency which will affect work schedules and work reviews. Employees may be asked to grow in very specific ways, whether these are stated explicitly or not.

The Manager's Three Choices

It should be clear at this point that a manager basically has three choices for factoring climate into employee development goals.

1. *Cope with existing conditions.* The manager who decides to accept conditions as they are identifies those factors which are pretty much fixed or "given" (laws, company philosophy and practices, customer require-

ments) and those which he determines are currently sound (scope of work, money and manpower budget, associates). The employee's development goals will then represent not only improvement in certain work but also improvement in that work under conditions which are likely to continue for the foreseeable future.

The engineering administration specialist in Chapter III listed as a work goal a revision in a technical manpower inventory for which he was responsible. Specifically, he thought that if technical employees coded their own work experience, there would be fewer errors in translating from the completed information forms to the punched card. This represents a good—that is, a needed, specific, measurable—work goal. The employee perhaps should learn something about programming, about coding. He should work on form building. He should develop a method for instructing technical personnel how to code the information. All the skill and knowledge he gains will be valuable both to him and to the firm since there will undoubtedly be other occasions for applying them in the future. His manager is not, however, asking of him more than the usual growth in knowledge expected of most employees. This is a fairly commonplace kind of development goal.

Suppose now the manager adds the situational context. This involves knowing what the working climate is like in the engineering department. For illustrative purposes, assume that the technical organizations are indifferent to or even resentful of administrative work. They typically delay it as long as possible. The managers place no importance on this kind of activity and base no part of their reward or recognition of individual effort on administrative accomplishment, especially when initiated outside their organizations.

In view of this attitude, the manpower inventory

improvement goal takes on new dimensions. Meeting it successfully under these conditions in all probability means acquiring relationship and communication skills of a high order which will add greatly to the administration specialist's qualifications for many positions. The development goal is no longer pedestrian but is, in fact, demanding. It will need exploration, discussion, and constructive planning on the part of both the administrative specialist and the manager of engineering.

2. *Cope with changing conditions.* Working within the context of existing conditions may be difficult, but it is not nearly so difficult as anticipating change and adapting to it. This adjustment to change represents the second opportunity for making development goals more incisive.

For example, the manager of a small business who has successfully invented a new product, seen it through all its initial difficulties, and finally debugged it is now ready to launch the product on the market. He is faced with dramatic changes in operations. Probably he must enlarge his production facilities, add to the number of hourly employees, and work out standard processes for manufacturing the new product so that cost will be competitive and quality uniformly high. These and other necessary changes represent good—needed, specific, measurable—work goals for individual employees. Further, the manager probably must alter the organization of his company to accommodate the new work, and this will mean changing long-time working relationships among employees. He probably must also concentrate, at least temporarily, less on design and development and more on production, promotion, and sales, and this will have a noticeable impact on parts of the organization which have been accustomed to a large share of his time and attention. If he anticipates these changes in time, begins to identify for employees the goal of working effectively within the new situation, and, of course, draws up sound plans to meet that goal, he will greatly decrease the odds that the changes will be disruptive. At very least he will cut down the time needed for adjustment.

And change need not be so dramatic. If production work done this year within a given budget must be done next year with 25 percent less money, the foreman's goals should be formulated to reflect the decrease in funds. If a salesman is faced with a new competitor in his area, his goals should reflect plans to meet and beat this competitor. It is the change in conditions that gives such work goals their development focus.

3. *Change conditions to meet development needs.* What is the third opportunity for capitalizing on situational factors to promote employee development? A deliberate change in working conditions.

Frequently, advancement up the organization lad-

Opportunities to Make Development Goals More Incisive

With respect to the working environment or situation, a manager may, with an individual employee or group of employees,

1. Set goals to cope with the existing situation.

2. Set goals to cope with an anticipated change in the situation.

3. Change the situation without changing work standards in order to provide greater development opportunity.

der means ability to do much the same work under much tougher conditions or under conditions of much greater decision-making freedom. Perhaps for this reason "flexibility" is often named as a broad development target for an individual. When we try to pin down exactly what is meant by the term, it seems to mean increased ability to work under a wide range of conditions. The usual way of developing this ability is job rotation—moving the individual around so that he is tried under a variety of managers, in a variety of different climates, and in association with a variety of other employees. This is a perfectly sound method of development, but it is usually possible for only a few individuals—the upper 5 to 10 percent of "promotables."

The manager who sees a development need of this kind in some or all of the employees need not limit himself to the "few." It is perfectly possible for him to take important, meaningful steps within his own organization to gain much of what broader job-rotation schemes accomplish. Say a vice president has reporting to him a personnel manager who is doing an excellent job of meeting the "people" needs of the business. For promotion to another, more important position in a different part of the firm, he will need to display the same ability but will probably have fewer employees to assist in getting results and a tighter budget. In this situation, the vice president can deliberately reduce the personnel manager's resources without lowering his standards. He will formulate goals in the same work-accomplishment terms as before but make clear the different conditions under which he expects them to be met.

In another instance, a manager may feel that an accountant is becoming too dependent on him for results. If he is wise, he deliberately changes the frequency of his contacts with the man in order to permit more freedom of decision making and encourage greater independent action. Needless to say, such a change in working conditions requires mental preparation and thoughtful timing. Usually a series of discussions with the employee is necessary to make sure that he understands the reasons for the change, and that both agree to the need for it and accept it.

Aids to Sound Judgments About Climate

Needless to say, also, the manager must make sound judgments about an existing or changing environment and its impact on employee output. Unfortunately, his ability to make appraisals in such areas may be hampered by two facts: (1) He is personally involved in the situation and may not be able to see it clearly. (2) It may well be the employee's perception of the situation that counts rather than the manager's view of it or even the situation itself.

The manager is really the key to the working climate. It is he who devises and effects the organization; it is he who sets the standards and rewards for output or penalizes lack of achievement; it is he who sets the tone for relationships and communication. It is he who interprets his own manager's policies, his company's philosophies, his associates' attitudes and viewpoints. It is he who reacts to competitors' actions, to economic conditions, to relevant legislation. Because of his involvement he may need the help of a third party—a staff man, an organization specialist, someone from the personnel department or from headquarters, an outside consultant—to collect objective information on which to base his appraisal of individual or total climate factors.

Moreover, in many instances the factual environment —the real organization structure, the actual pressure for results, the true deadline, the resources actually available—matters very little. It is the employee's perception of what these are that counts. If the manager believes he is emphasizing quality of product above all else and the inspection force believes that cost, cost, cost is what he is preaching, lower cost is what the manager will get and quality may suffer. In evaluating climate, therefore, the manager needs information both about the facts of the situation and about the employee's perception of it. What tools are available for these purposes?

The individual employee interview. This is not a formal, elaborate tool. The manager preferably takes advantage of a normal work discussion or of a work planning or performance appraisal feedback session to explore with the employee his reactions to the environment in which he is working. Is his schedule too tight, too easy, or about right? Is he getting enough overall information? What about quality standards he is expected to meet? Do there seem to be organization bottlenecks? From a discussion of such subjects as these, the manager gets insights into climate as the employee responds to it. Naturally, frankness of response is limited by the basic relationship between the two men and by the employee's past favorable or unfavorable experience in discussions with his manager. However, the information to be gained is useful, and the employee's performance should be considered in the light of his reaction to the context of his job.

The analytical study. Certain environmental factors such as organization, information flow, and schedules lend themselves to factual data collection and analysis. Assignment of an individual or a team of individuals to study the situation—to interview appropriate employees, gather information on work flow, observe work in process, and then analyze the picture—is valuable, both for the manager who needs the information and, as a learning experience, for those named to the project. The information collected, together with recommendations for desirable changes, provides a base for managerial decision making.

The attitude or opinion survey. Surveys or polls have been popular in recent years, particularly as a means of obtaining information on employee attitudes. These rely on prepared questions which are answered by the employees during an oral interview or anonymously in writing. All employees or only a representative sample may be included.

Oral surveys are best conducted by professionals who have special training in interview techniques and in the recording of information in predetermined ways. In all surveys, such matters as the size of the sample, the design of the questions, the gradations of choice, and provision for easy hand or machine scoring require professional know-how. Even more important, the analysis and interpretation of employee replies require considerable experience and skill if useful conclusions are to be reached. For these a manager should seek the help of a competent adviser from the personnel organization or an outside agency.

Survey data are subjective opinions. They represent a view of the situation, not necessarily facts. The manager needs to keep this in mind so that any action he takes as a result of a survey will reflect his understanding of the pitfalls involved. Since, however, the device has high potential if well handled, here are a few suggestions:

Before the survey:

1. Don't make a survey unless action will be taken as a result of it.

Appraising the Situation

Climate or Environment	Key Factors	Tools for Appraisal
Internal	Organization Resources Work Schedules Communication, Information Managing Style	Individual Employee Interview Study Attitude or Opinion Survey Oral Written Devices for Upward Communication Questions, Comments from Employee Meetings Grievance Procedure Suggestion System
External	Company as a Whole: Philosophy Objectives Policies Strategy Business, Industry: Traditions Practices Customer Requirements Competition Government, Economic, Cultural Influences	Company as a Whole: Information from Manager's Manager Company Meetings Company Publications Announced Company Business Plans Business, Industry: Market Research Data Marketing, Sales Organizations Trade Association Meetings Business and Trade Journals Personal Contacts Government, Economic, Cultural: Consultants Newspapers, Magazines, Journals Lectures, Courses Special Reading Personal Travel Observations

2. Reach agreement with the managers of all employees who will be surveyed on the areas to be explored and limit survey content to a few important questions.

3. Make sure all managers agree ahead of time on the wording of questions to be asked and that each selects what appears to him to be the "right" response to each question about his work area and its climate. Managers have a way of rationalizing employee responses if this step is not taken in advance.

4. Agree to keep responses anonymous; don't try to identify respondents no matter how tempting this may be.

5. Pave the way with participating employees; tell them what will be done with the information.

After the survey:

1. Feed back factual results and intended action at least to participating managers and employees —and do it quickly.

2. Express gratitude for the negative or unfavorable responses as well as for the favorable ones; otherwise employees will not cooperate next time.

3. Accept responses in the light of current events but don't assume that an unfavorable reaction will disappear if action is taken to eliminate certain conditions.

4. Take promised action quickly, involving all affected managers in planning what needs to be done.

5. Make another survey after a reasonable period (6 to 12 months) to see whether the action taken has had any impact.

The survey of employee opinion, if it is well done and if individual anonymity is preserved, is one of the few tools which supplies useful information about working environment *even if the climate is poor.*

Devices for upward communication. Upward communication is a sort of catch-all phrase covering a wide variety of devices intended to encourage employees to let managers know what is on their minds. Most fall into one of two categories: (1) meetings in which there is opportunity for either anonymous or identifiable comment or questions and (2) procedures whereby an employee who has a grievance or a suggestion can make this known without necessarily being limited to his immediate supervisor or manager.

If meetings are carefully structured so that employees know the topic under consideration in advance, if devices such as buzz sessions or small group discussions are employed to supplement the larger meeting, if time is given to prepare questions or comments, a manager can often identify employee reaction to environmental factors. It is unfortunately true, however, that when the climate is good, the best information is obtained; when the climate is poor, the least trustworthy is usually volunteered.

Suggestion systems, grievance procedures, and similar means of putting higher-level managers in touch with individual employees may help solve individual employee problems, but they are only occasionally of use in helping the manager appraise the total environment.

The big picture. It is not enough for a manager to be systematic in analyzing the internal climate of the organization. He must also be alert to events and influences outside his control which affect the total working environment in essential ways. Much of this area is outside the scope of this book. It is perhaps sufficient to say that a manager should not wait to be informed but should actively seek needed information. Knowledge of the firm comes from his own manager, from company meetings and publications, from announced business plans. Knowledge of the business or industry is obtained from market research data, marketing or sales personnel, business and trade journals, and, of course, personal contacts with customers or dealers or distributors. Knowledge of government, economic, and cultural conditions may be available from specialists, from selected reading and courses, and from the manager's own travel observations.

Climate, then, is not the vague intangible thing it is sometimes made to appear. It is the product of some quite specific management practices and devices. With the help of the available tools, a manager can examine them, appraise them, and make decisions about maintaining, interpreting, or changing them based on their impact on individual and organization performance results. He then factors his decisions into the needed work improvement goals, keeping in mind that these may be

... for an individual or an organization or

... for current or future work improvements and may involve

... coping with existing conditions,

... coping with anticipated changes, or

... deliberately changing conditions for sound reasons.

In any event, if they are to produce development, they must require *adding knowledge or skill or changing values or attitudes in a needed, important way.*

CHAPTER V

BUILDING ON INDIVIDUAL
TALENT AND MOTIVATION

Manager x is serious about employee development. He looks at the long-range commitments of his department. He compares actual performance with what is needed. He identifies clear-cut opportunities for preparing for the future and for improving output now. He factors in the situation or climate in which work must be done. Having taken all these steps, however, he is not quite ready to negotiate specific development goals with employees. For there remains the task of understanding individual talents, interests, and career objectives so that agreed-upon development goals are within employee abilities and accomplishment is compatible with fundamental interests.

This requires a third set of appraisals—difficult appraisals—on the manager's part. Many of the tools currently favored for the purpose require special training to use and interpret. Past experience has shown frequent errors in predicting what a given employee will be able to do several years from now. It is, therefore, unusually important to understand how to use the available tools for appraising present and potential ability, to recognize their limitations and the resulting need for supplementary devices, and to make frequent use of professional advice and the help of the employee himself.

What are these major tools and how can a manager take advantage of them to acquire much needed information?

Personal History Analysis

Psychologists say that the best predictor of what an individual will do in the future is what he has done in the past—if, of course, we assume reasonable similarity of action and conditions. The manager who wishes to estimate what critical choices an employee will make in the years ahead, how he will grow, and what will motivate him should therefore explore his past behavior systematically. There are two logical sources of the necessary information: personnel records and the personal interview.

Record analysis. Every firm maintains some basic historical data on its employees. The record may consist of a completed application blank, a résumé submitted for employment purposes, or an information form for the company's skills register or inventory. It usually contains the pertinent facts about age, educational history, and employment history (including salary, although the payroll record probably gives more specific detail on increases awarded at various points in time). It may occasionally cover career goals, job interests, and extracurricular activities. In addition, the personnel file is very likely to include ratings or appraisals made by

Appraisal of Talent and Motivation

(Man-Manager Interview)

Prerequisites:

1. Recognition of information as employee's view of it.

2. Man-manager relationship of mutual respect and confidence.

3. Managerial openmindedness.

4. Managerial skill as interviewer.

Specific Information to Explore:

1. Responsibilities of each position:

    a. What experiences and learning gained?

    b. What difficulties? How much effort required?

    c. What likes and dislikes?

    d. What helps and hindrances from environmental factors?

    e. Reward — or lack of it?

2. Changes in position, interests, or personal goals:

    a. What reasons for decision?

    b. Who contributed to decision?

3. Focus of current career goals:

    a. Next jobs rather than single ultimate job.

    b. Development opportunities in current job useful in several next possible jobs.

various managers, representing their opinion of the employee's work at the time of evaluation.

The manager reviews the personal history and translates it into a current picture of the knowledge, skill, experience, and demonstrated interests of the employee. He looks for inconsistencies in the record—gaps in employment and shifts in career direction, outside activities, or educational efforts—since these may indicate self-recognition of talent deficiencies for certain kinds of work, new interests, or changed thinking with respect to ultimate goals. For example, an engineer who moves to a manufacturing assignment and later to a marketing one may have decided that he is not as strong technically as he would like to be. Or he may have concluded that he would like to run a business one day and needs the broadening experience of getting to know several company functions.

The manager makes a special note of how rapidly the employee's salary has increased and how long he has remained on various jobs before going on to better ones; these are objective indications of how previous managers viewed the man's performance. Obviously, though, these factors cannot be considered in isolation. If the total economy was poor, or if the company was in bad shape during a given period, this may explain small or slow increases and fewer promotions. If, on the other hand, the business was new and was growing rapidly, greater advancement than normal would probably have occurred.

Of special significance are the written performance appraisals. The current manager reads these carefully, noting what the employee appears to have done well consistently, what he has consistently done poorly, and what trends or changes have marked his working career. Statements by former bosses have their limitations, naturally, since in all probability the reader has no way of knowing their standards, but he can at least look for points of agreement among them.

The sum of the record material provides a "snapshot" of the employee's current qualifications. Steady growth in experience, in capabilities, in expressed interests, and in career pattern are a basis for the prediction of continued success in the future.

Interview data analysis. The analysis of the personnel record, accurate and factual though it may be, demands that the manager read between the lines and speculate on the reasons for changes. The inferences he draws may be grossly in error. Record analysis therefore needs to be supplemented with additional information, and the logical source for it—in many cases the only source—is the employee. So the manager interviews the employee, recognizing certain limitations inherent in this process also.

First of all, information obtained by this method represents, at best, the picture as seen through the employee's eyes. Second, the employee-manager relationship needs to be one of mutual respect and confidence if the discussion is to evoke an honest view. Third, the manager must suspend judgment—keep an open mind—about the employee's motives, abilities, and potential if he is to hear all the employee says. Finally, the manager must be skillful in interviewing, and the occasion must be reasonably free of outside pressures if it is to be fully revealing.

The objective of the interview, of course, is not to repeat information already available in the records but, rather, to explore in a more detailed way the experiences and learning gained, the difficulties and the effort required, the likes and dislikes, the environment with its helps and hindrances, and the reward or lack of it in carrying out key work assignments. As each change in position, interest, or goal comes to light, the manager probes to learn the reason for the change and the factors contributing to it—wife, manager, associates, personal feeling.

Because the information thus obtained is subjective, the manager may wish to verify certain critical points with former managers or employers. To complete the picture, he needs additional information from the employee about his current career objectives. This area is best explored by emphasizing only lightly the ultimate or highest-level position to which the employee may aspire and stressing possible next positions more heavily. Another slightly different approach is to ask the employee which of the jobs he sees around him—jobs, that is, with which he is at least somewhat familiar— seem to be ones he would like to be doing in the near future or within a year or two.

The manager has a number of tasks during this part of the interview. He must relate what the employee has already told him about past learning, likes, successes, rewards, and reasons for change to the expressed career goals. Are these consistent and realistic? If not, the manager should obviously not argue or try to lower the employee's sights. Instead, he should explore the reasons for inconsistencies, provide any facts he has about anticipated business changes, explain what compensation is attached to the various positions discussed, and the like. The employee is then able to factor the information into his thinking in the way he feels is warranted. If he admits he doesn't know what he wants to do in the future, the manager shouldn't criticize this lack of direction; rather, he might suggest a range of possibilities based on his observations of the employee and what the employee has told him. Certainly he should be prepared to describe the company's plans, at least for the immediate future, together with their implications for manpower needs. In this way, the employee is able to fit himself into a more realistic framework; he won't simply be evolving vague schemes of "where he wants to go."

There are some dangers, true, in discussing careers. If the employee is not on top of his current job, he may be distracted from improving on presently assigned work. He may even view the discussion as a more or less subtle suggestion that the manager is not satisfied and feels he would be better off elsewhere. So the manager who probes for career goals should limit himself to employees who have been on their present jobs long enough, and are performing them well enough, that an upward or broadening move is a reasonable possibility within the foreseeable future.

Moreover, an employee's interests change with time, as do the business and its environment. Opportunities not envisioned by either manager or employee today may open up tomorrow. For this reason too, it is desirable to keep career goals focused on the near future, on *next* jobs, and to direct any development efforts toward skills and experience which are likely to be needed in a variety of positions.

A third danger is that, having gone on record with his manager about his ambitions, and having heard the manager describe the company's plans with their implied opportunities, the employee may feel that the manager owes him advancement along the lines discussed. The manager must therefore make it clear that he will do everything within reason to help the employee build certain development goals into his present position, but that future openings will be filled on a competitive basis. To whatever extent the employee is able to acquire needed know-how, he will have an

advantage. Since promotion cannot be assured, however, he should share in discussions about his development goals so that he is aware of any risks involved and
is willing to undertake them.

If the relationship between employee and manager
is not a sound one, or if the manager does not possess
the interviewing skill required to do a good job of getting the necessary information, the services of a professional interviewer should be employed. This might
be an individual in the personnel office, a representative of company headquarters (in the larger company),
or an outside consultant with a management consulting
firm, a college or university, or a local service agency.
When the employee approaches such an adviser on his
own, he can of course control the information given his
manager or supervisor. But, if it is a company-sponsored
session, ethics demand that the employee know in
advance what information will be given his manager or
the personnel department and so become a matter of
record.

Observation of Employee Behavior

Most managers observe the employee at work and in
various social situations without prompting; in fact, they
base much of their intuitive employee appraisal on their
observations. To make their findings really useful for
predicting future growth, however, they need to follow
a five-point procedure. (See Suggested Form 6 for a
possible format.)

1. Document the nature of the occasion.
2. Document the situation or climate in which it
   occurred.
3. Describe the employee's behavior, including any
   changes exhibited as the situation changed.

SUGGESTED FORM 6

DOCUMENTATION OF EMPLOYEE BEHAVIOR

Employee: _____ Date: _____

Manager: _____

1. Describe the occasion on which employee was observed:

2. What was the employee's role? Participant, leader, observer?

3. Describe influencing conditions. (Consider those present, time or timing, pressures, what was to be accomplished, structure.)

4. Describe employee's behavior. (What did he do and say, how did others respond, what was employee's reaction to others' response?)

5. Did any changes in behavior occur on this occasion? If so, what appeared to cause the change?

6. Have you observed the employee on similar occasions? If so, was his behavior approximately the same or different? If different, in what ways? What seemed to cause the difference?

4. Repeat frequently enough to get a reasonable sample of behavior.

5. Look for consistencies and trends in the data over an extended period of time.

Document the occasion. Don't be misled by the word "document." This simply means jotting down a few written notes which state the kind of event during which the employee was observed. For example, a staff meeting at which his associates were present. Or a presentation of a contract proposal to an important customer. Or a work review conference with his manager during which he reported on progress with no one else present.

Document the situation. Make notes of factors which may have affected or influenced the employee's actions. For example, was the staff meeting a relaxed information exchange, or did something occur to put the man under pressure? If so, what was it? At the customer presentation, were high-level managers present? Was the customer receptive, cool, or critical? And so on.

Describe employee behavior. Record the highlights. The employee was calm and convincing when questioned. He failed to participate in the meeting, was quiet but interested. Note any changes. For example, in the beginning he was quite thorough and deliberate in his approach, but as the deadline neared, he became hurried and somewhat irritated.

Repeat frequently. It seems obvious that observations must be made often enough to discount the nonrepresentative behavior which occasionally occurs if a person is overtired, is not feeling well, has problems at home, or whatever. Even "stray" behavior contributes to the total picture, however, when the condition which produced it can be identified.

Look for consistencies and trends. These, remember, are the basis for prediction. If the employee consistently

fails to participate in large groups but is fluent in two-
to three-man meetings, the manager can conclude that
large groups represent a problem for the employee and,
perhaps, depending on other circumstances, a development goal. If the employee shows great nervousness in
early meetings with top company executives but is
more and more at ease with them as time goes on, the
manager is fairly safe in predicting that this will not be
a problem area for the employee in the future. He may
want to see whether the employee shows the same
reaction to first meetings with everyone or whether only
higher-level managers make him nervous, but this is
easily checked out.

Behavior observation supplies the most useful information if a manager has clearly in mind tentative work
improvement goals which need to be met under certain
conditions. He can then observe the employee doing
comparable work in similar situations and thus determine the extent to which the goals are within the
employee's ability and how much development will be
required in order to master the needed skills. For
example, take the engineering administration specialist
who felt self-coding of experience inventory forms by
technical personnel would reduce card-punching errors.
Knowing that the engineers were indifferent at best to
administrative projects of this sort, his manager might
have set up a meeting on some other paperwork matter,
given the specialist the task of convincing the engineering managers, and observed how he handled the
situation. He might have taken advantage of staff meetings in this way on three or four occasions. The administration specialist's behavior, and especially the
improvement in his behavior as he began to understand
and react to the problem facing him, would have given
his manager important evidence on the soundness of

the development goal he was considering—in this case, the self-coding of the inventory forms.

Appraisal of Potential

Many firms ask managers to make a periodic appraisal of each employee's potential in connection with the employee's performance appraisal—probably on an annual basis. If potential is appraised separately, the job is probably done every two to three years. (See Suggested Form 7 for a possible format.)

Essentially, an appraisal of potential requires that a manager review his analysis of the employee's work record to pinpoint special areas of knowledge and know-how of value to the company now and in the future. He goes over his interview notes to single out things the employee likes to do, the sorts of rewards he is seeking in his career, and the career interests or goals toward which he is willing to work. In addition, the manager points to behavior which might qualify the employee to handle certain work situations under various conditions. He bases his projections both on present abilities and behavior and on trends exhibited over the years to estimate growth in certain directions and "plateauing" or deterioration in others.

Appraisals of potential are more likely to be accurate if potential for "what" is identified; that is, if the employee is considered as a candidate for several different future jobs rather than for growth in general. It helps, too, if one employee is compared with another in terms of relative qualifications for a given job and if the judgments of several managers who have had an opportunity to know the employee and see his work can be pooled. Because of this pooling, as well as any trends they may show, successive appraisals of potential over the years provide a more helpful base for prediction than a single appraisal. And, since appraisal information is subject to individual interpretation, and since managers faced with the same evidence may predict quite different growth patterns, it is helpful if the data or evidence used can be included in the record.

In an effort to reconcile various managerial judgments, a third party—a member of the personnel organization, for example—is sometimes asked to obtain the needed data by interviewing managers, either individually or in a group. Through skillful questioning he is often able to find a basis for reaching certain conclusions about the employee. Then, he either makes the reconciliation himself, using his professional judgment, or helps the managers in the group to reach a consensus. This method is sometimes known as field review.

Tests and Their Value

Psychologists, over the years, have recognized the limitations of managerial appraisals of employee capacity based solely on what can be learned from seeing the employee at work and in various other situations and from what he is willing to reveal about himself. Therefore, they have developed tests to sample certain areas of employee knowledge, skill, behavior, attitude, personality, values, and interests under standard conditions. These provide additional information which can be factored into a manager's judgment.

Tests do, however, usually require trained administrators in order to preserve standard, and therefore comparable, performance conditions. They always require professional interpretation of findings. Most tests are based on statistical analysis; thus a favorable score can

SUGGESTED FORM 7

APPRAISAL OF EMPLOYEE POTENTIAL

Employee: _____ Manager: _____

Position: _____ Date: _____

In answering each of the questions below, cite specific evidence used to reach your conclusions.

1. What are the employee's major talents on which to build? (Consider knowledge, skill, specific experience, ability to handle certain kinds of situations, and so on.)

2. What major untested areas should be explored? (Consider knowledge, skill, specific experience, ability to handle certain kinds of situations, and so on.)

3. What seem to be fields of work or work situations to be avoided? (List only areas which seem to represent significant deficiencies related to likely career progress.)

4. What are the employee's likes and dislikes so far as his present work is concerned?

5. Does the employee have career goals toward which he is working? What are his reasons for them?

6. Do the employee's career goals seem realistic or not? Why? Are there others which seem more suitable?

7. What appear to be reasonable next jobs for the employee? Would these represent broadening experiences or advancement? How soon do you estimate the employee would be ready for each? What preparations, if any, would he have to make?

be said only to increase the chances that the employee knows this or that, or is like this or that, or would behave in this or that fashion. Even so, they may yield information which would otherwise not be available.

Kinds of tests. Tests of *achievement* essentially ask questions which determine what the employee has learned about a given field or learned to do in a given skill area. For example, an algebra test gives, on a sample basis, an index of knowledge of algebra; a driver's test gives, on a sample basis, an index of driving ability. An *aptitude* test is designed to give an index of a person's talent in an area not yet much studied or used. For example, an engineering aptitude test may tell a high school student of his probable talents for engineering even though he has never had an engineering course. Probably the most useful of the aptitude tests for adults who are already in the midst of their careers is the so-called *intelligence* test, which indicates the ability of the person to learn. The rest would seem to be most valuable for student vocational counseling.

Then there are *personality, interest,* and *attitude* tests. The paper-and-pencil, self-report type asks a variety of questions which the employee is expected to answer candidly. The employee's answers are compared with norm groups, and on this basis he is judged to have certain characteristics, be interested in certain fields, or possess certain attitudes or values. Because of their dependence on honesty, these tests' usefulness is limited except when the employee asks for help and, therefore, is more likely to be truthful in his replies. The *projective* type of test requires the employee to examine relatively unstructured materials and describe what he sees, draw a picture with the help of rather incomplete instructions, or make up a story based on a picture. From his responses a trained psychologist builds a description of the employee's basic personality characteristics. Projective tests are usually administered and always interpreted on an individual basis; they depend heavily on the skill of the psychologist for their validity.

A very popular device today is the group *situational* test. Usually several individuals are placed in a "situation," given a problem to solve, and turned loose on it. The situation may be relatively unstructured so as to provide considerable freedom of individual behavior, or it may be structured so that the role of each member of the group is prescribed. Various pressures may be developed—time limitations, competition between groups, and similar factors. Observers note the behavior exhibited under different conditions and in different roles. They watch to see whether the individual typically assumes a given role if he has a choice, whether he performs this well, how he performs in other roles perhaps not chosen but imposed on him, and how he responds to varying types of pressure.[1]

There are a number of obvious problems connected with such testing. The observers of the test must be able to reach some consensus about the participating individuals. Moreover, an individual needs to exhibit at least some consistency of behavior or, if his behavior is inconsistent, then the differences should be traceable to changes in the imposed conditions.

The situational test need not be performed in a group, although the opportunity to observe behavior in a group is very desirable. Individual *situational* tests are also popular. The so-called stress interview in which the interviewer deliberately imposes stress conditions on the interviewee by arguing with him, contradicting him, and

[1] For a brief description of AT&T's use of situational testing in its Assessment Center Program see "The Hard Look in Employee Appraisal," *Dun's Review and Modern Industry*, September 1966.

so on is clearly such a test, providing indications of the interviewee's probable reactions in similar circumstances. So is the in-basket test,[2] in which the subject is given a variety of materials simulating those which might appear in the daily in-basket of the manager whose role he is "playing." The subject then, under certain restrictions of timing, handles each item as carefully as he might if he were confronted with it in real life.

There is a certain face validity about situational testing which has a great deal of appeal. The problems to be solved can be chosen for their likeness to problems faced on the day-to-day job. The roles played—manager, information supplier, decision maker, and so on—are typical. And there is an additional valuable by-product. If managers are asked to help observe along with test experts, their understanding of the individuals being tested is likely to improve as well as their skill in observing behavior.

Testing terms managers need to understand. Managers should be knowledgeable about a number of points in order to use test information responsibly in appraising employee talent and potential. They should know, first of all, whether a test is reasonably *reliable*; that is, if the person were to take the same test again, memory factor aside, is he likely to get about the same score? If the answer is no, the test results are obviously meaningless and cannot be used.

Managers should know how *valid* a given test is; that is, does it measure what it purports to measure? No test does this perfectly for an individual since it is, after all, a sampling technique based on group data, but the odds should be in favor of its doing what it says it does.

---

[2] For an excellent description of the in-basket test, see Lopez, Felix M., Jr., *Evaluating Executive Decision Making: The In-Basket Technique,* AMA Research Study 75, 1966.

What is, or was, the *norm group?* That is, against the performance of what kind of people was the test validated? (If it was a test of creativity and was validated against the scores of a group of accountants, it is unlikely to be useful in predicting the creativity of engineers.) The manuals of all reputable test publishers supply such information, so that the administrator should be able to answer the manager's questions.

Managers should also understand what is meant by *percentiles.* Most test scores are given in percentile terms, meaning that the employee's score was placed in rank order with scores of other individuals and converted into a number indicating the percentage of other scores he equals or exceeds. A score at the 60th percentile, then, is quite good, indicating that he equals or beats 60 percent of those who took the same test. It is sometimes hard for managers to think this way—they tend to remember a 60 percent mark in school as being poor.

How to work with professional testers. For maximum benefit from test information, a manager needs to work closely with the professional tester. One good way to do this is to review what is known about the employee's talents and interests with the professional and ask for his help in areas where there is conflicting evidence or for which there is very little evidence. The test administrator will then be in a position to advise what information tests are likely to add and point out, as well, areas in which tests are not likely to be useful or will be of limited usefulness.

When tests have been administered and the results are known, the test interpreter can help the manager fit the data into what he knew previously about the employee and suggest ways to resolve any new contradictions which may have developed. He does this by

examining the evidence on which the conflicting conclusions were reached in an effort to find other influences which may have affected the findings. Only when
test data are factored in this way into the total evaluation picture is the manager's appraisal of the employee's capabilities and probable growth potential enriched.

A well-conceived and professionally administered testing program is an asset to a company, its managers, and
its employees. All concerned, however, need to understand the purpose of the program, the advantages and
limitations of the tests, and the use which will be made
of the results. Employees should have feedback on their
test performance so that they can add it to their self-
appraisal for development planning purposes. And they
should have full assurance that the test data will be
available only to those who have reason to use them
and who understand how to use them properly.

The Computer: Its Contribution

Until quite recently, a manager who carefully collected information about employee performance under
varying conditions and attempted to predict future
growth was usually in an awkward position from two
points of view. First of all, past appraisals were scantily
documented, if at all, and then in quite general terms;
the information they contained was not very useful as a
base for prediction. Once the manager had done his
best to put together the data he needed to estimate
potential, he had to develop a system for keeping it
current; otherwise "the wheel had to be reinvented"
each time serious talent appraisal was undertaken.

The availability today of computer storage and computer analysis of data removes many of these former

difficulties. Certainly factual information, once obtained, need not be gathered again. The basic data on education, experience, test results, and the like can safely be stored for use as required. Specific behavioral and skill information also can be stored, together with situational influences. Aided by a computer programmer, the manager can work with the machine to find trends in employee performance and behavior; and these, in turn, can help him predict likely performance and behavior in specified future jobs—given, of course, certain interim experiences and training and certain assumptions about continuance of trends.[3]

There is a tendency to think of the computer as an impractical tool for managers to use in personnel matters—one which, besides, is available only in larger companies. The truth is that almost all businesses today, regardless of size, are making use of the computer for payroll and other accounting functions, for inventory and other production control systems, and for engineering analyses of all kinds. The personnel function has lagged in its use. The availability of time-sharing arrangements with remote access to computer centers places the computer within reach of individual managers as well as personnel organizations.

The biggest problem remains that of deciding what information should be stored in the computer, since that information's accuracy and relevance determine how well future data can be supplied on request and predictions made which are reliable and valid. Beyond the standard education, skills, test data, and experience categories, this list has been proposed for managers:[4]

---

[3] For a provocative discussion of the possibilities opened by innovative computer usage, see Ferguson, Lawrence L., "Better Management of Managers' Careers," *Harvard Business Review*, March-April 1966.

[4] Ferguson, *ibid.*

— What they actually *do* in their various jobs.
— What methods they use.
— What the situational factors are which surround their successes and failures.
— How they make decisions and implement them.
— What opportunities they have to make mistakes.
— What results (good or bad) they achieve.
— What other factors impinge on individual managerial effectiveness.

It is a good list, and its application extends beyond the managerial group of employees to employees generally.

Managers, then, as well as personnel organizations, should be aware of the potential assistance of the computer in helping make more accurate appraisals of employee capabilities, more likely appraisals of potential, and more realistic employee development plans.

* * *

Having made his appraisal of the employee's talents and interests, on the basis of considerable information from the employee himself and with professional and computer help as needed and available, the manager now turns back to the problem of finalizing employee development goals. From his analysis of current commitments and future plans he has tentatively identified a range of goals which, if achieved, would be of value to the business. He has analyzed the climate or environment and added this element in with the rest to make the goals more incisive. Now he has the opportunity to reflect the employee's talents and purposes so as to hold forth personal rewards and thus provide incentive for extra effort.

In making this final incorporation, there are several fundamentals to guide the manager:

1. Build on strengths.
2. Build on likes.

3. Make development goals compatible with career interests.

4. Work in the shorter range.

Build on strengths. Development goals, we have said, should be based on people's strengths, not their weaknesses. Sometimes this is misinterpreted to mean that growth occurs only in those areas where strength has already been exhibited. This is far from true. Ignorance can be remedied by study; inexperience can be overcome by practice. In fact, areas such as these may represent very strong growth opportunities.

What we mean is that the chances of success are greater if we use and develop our talents and that, conversely, we are least likely to grow in those areas for which we have little or no talent and where, indeed, we have real deficiencies. For a person to attempt to be a singer if he is tone-deaf, for example, is an impossible task. Or, if an individual has little or no gift for mathematics—not because he has never studied math or tried to use it but, rather, because he has tried it and has learned that with the same effort he does much better in, say, English or history—it is probably wiser for him to choose a career requiring English than one requiring math. Even then, caution is the word, since there is always the individual who, like Demosthenes, is so determined to overcome a handicap that he does. But, for the manager who is trying to help an individual select reasonable targets or goals for development, the soundest action is to identify known talents or strengths (things the individual does well) along with the "unknowns" (things the individual doesn't know whether he can do well or not because he hasn't tried them); rather than search for known deficiencies to correct or change and make them the focus for development effort.

Suppose, for example, that *Henry Ardin* is poor at

detailed clerical work. He is, however, an excellent consumer products salesman. In working with Henry, Manager A will do better to select development goals that relate to selling difficult customers or dealers and improving the volume sales of lagging products than to focus Henry's efforts on record keeping and reporting. Chances are the payoff to the company and to Henry will be higher.

Build on likes. Psychologists tell us there is a high correlation between what we like to do and what we do well. Again, this doesn't mean that, if an employee

Appraising Individual Talent and Interest

Tools for Information Collection and Analysis	Opportunities to Strengthen Development Goals
Personal History Analysis Personnel Records Personal Interview	Build on Strengths
Observation of Employee Behavior	Build on Likes
Appraisal of Potential Field Review	Match Career Goals
Tests Achievement Aptitude Self-Report Personality, Attitude, Interest, Values Projective Situational Group Individual	Work in the Shorter Range Identify Goals in Current Work Use in Near Future
The Computer Information Storage Prediction	

has never tried something, he can be expected not to like it. But, if he has had a reasonable introduction to a given activity and has tried it a few times and doesn't like it, it is probably not an area in which he has great talent. If, too, he expresses an interest in management but has never managed anything, there is no reason to believe he will do it well. The principle simply holds that, if he likes to do something and has done it a fair number of times, the chances are he is good at it. In any event, expressed "likes" in education, work, and work approaches or methods are a source of sound development goals.

Take *Mary Brian* as an example. She is a payroll clerk, and the part of her job she likes best is setting up systems for short cuts and for checking the accuracy of her own work. These puzzles or problems interest her very much; she thinks about them on her way to work and talks about them with her associates at lunch. It would therefore be reasonable for her boss to explore with her the possibility of learning simple computer programming—provided, of course, she has the requisite educational background.

Make development goals compatible with career interests. It seems obvious that, if an employee has strong career interests, the manager should capitalize on these in building development goals. New knowledge, the need to cope with different conditions, many of the elements which make up the eventual job desired can be found within the current job. To help the employee see the relationship between his career objectives and the development goals he is being asked to achieve requires exploration and negotiation. Yet, once the relationship is seen, it should provide the employee with increased motivation to achieve the goals. It may be that a trade-off is desirable under certain conditions.

If the manager views the employee's career goals as realistic for him and of value to the firm, and if the employee's current assignment provides very little growth opportunity directed toward these stated goals, the manager may decide it is worth the investment of some of the employee's time in special assignments or task forces.

An obvious example of this principle in operation is that of the specialist *Al Taylor,* who wants to become a manager some day. Manager *B* may have no real evidence as to whether this is realistic or not. He sees, however, some things that can be built into Al's job immediately. He can, for example, ask him to prepare his own budget, he can give him more responsibility for representing the department before associates and higher-level managers, and he can ask him to pull together the plans for a particular project by consulting with everyone concerned. The employee's response in each case will give clues about his managerial potential. But the most fundamental management responsibility of all cannot be built into Al's present job—the responsibility for getting his work done through other people. So, if most signs thus far are favorable, Manager *B* may ask Al to substitute for him while he is on vacation, take a course or do some reading on management, or head up a special study on which others will work. These activities will allow Al to try himself as a manager and provide Manager *B* with evidence on which to make an eventual decision.

Work in the shorter range. Employee values and ambitions usually shift considerably with experience. Our ability to predict how an individual will respond to opportunities, apply new knowledge, and retain old interests becomes much poorer the further into the future we try to project his potential. Organizational plans and conditions also change with time. That is why, insofar as possible, it is best to emphasize interests, activity, and goals one or two years ahead rather than ten or twenty. Even then, breaking these into shorter-range subgoals is more likely to pay off. The manager sees to it that the employee is working on something in the real "here and now" rather than in the speculative future. In this way, application of what is learned is possible before the new knowledge or skill or interest is lost.

The employee who at age 24 says he wants eventually to be the firm's vice president in charge of sales is not likely to be greatly helped if his manager takes all the elements of the vice president's job and attempts to build a development plan around them. He will undoubtedly be of greater service to the employee if he helps identify some of the types of knowledge which might contribute to the ultimate goal—such as knowing customers, customer requirements, and company products better—incorporates one or two of these into the present job, and focuses the employee's attention squarely on doing outstanding sales work right now.

In summary, the manager must have a sound picture of the individual's talents and interests to add to his conclusions about needed performance improvements within the current or anticipated setting in which they must be made. Then and only then is he ready to establish employee development goals.

CHAPTER VI

CHOOSING AND ACCEPTING
DEVELOPMENT GOALS

WHILE THE AVAILABLE INFORMATION-GATHERING TOOLS supply the manager who wants to set sound development targets for a particular employee or group of employees with an attractive range of possibilities, none stands on its own merits.

If the manager finds that the work is new and challenging but the employee lacks talent for it, interest in it, or both, not much growth is likely to result. If it appears that the employee has the talent and the interest but the climate inhibits risk taking and rewards only those who never rock the boat, growth will probably be far below potential. And so, in the end, judgment must be used to insure favorable interaction among work, climate, and individual talent and interest.

There are few, if any, tools or guides to help the manager achieve a balanced judgment. In the firm with an established philosophy of employee development or, better still, a manpower development plan based on anticipated business needs, there may be a system of weights to assign various alternatives. Where the employee's present job offers important opportunities or the work of the organization is unusually challenging, current commitments may override other considerations.

The more normal situation, however, is that demands from all sides are so high that choice among them is difficult. The major hope for sound decision making is for the manager to use his information-gathering tools systematically and consider the individual merits of alternatives thoughtfully, so that in the end a happy marriage of the possibilities may be arrived at.

This process is actually no easier and no harder than deciding on business goals or work goals. Critical information or intelligence is gathered from the variety of sources we have described. It is weighed, analyzed, and integrated. Open courses of action are considered, and the final choice is based on assumptions, past experience, and, occasionally, the "gut feel" of a strong-minded individual.

But the number of goals must also be decided upon. How many are to be undertaken at any one time? This decision is necessarily affected by such factors as the urgency of the need for growth in certain areas, the maturity of the employee, the amount of change entailed, and the current workload. However, it is usually wiser to concentrate the employee's effort on one or two goals which are within his ability and offer potentially high payoff. Then, when he has had some success with these, he can go on to new goals. Allowing him to divide his attention among a large number of goals, all of which may be sound in themselves, may dissipate his energies and delay success so far into the future that both employee and manager lose interest.

How the Manager Reaches His Decision

Let's look at two typical situations to get a feeling for the decision-making process. Suppose Manager *X* has a man reporting to him named *Harvey Langley*. Harv is new to the job and the company but quite experienced in similar work. His current assignment carries responsibility for all the subcontracted manufacturing business of the firm. Manager X hired Harv because of his previous experience. He doesn't know what this new man's ultimate value may be to the company; but, since Harv's salary is high in comparison with that of associates at the same level in the organization, Manager X intends to enlarge Harv's responsibilities in time and, to this end, wants to establish proper development goals toward which Harv can work.

Manager X appraises the basic factors in individual goal setting: work and climate along with employee talent and interest. In the work area, Harv has a great deal to accomplish during the next half year or so. There are organization problems, procedures problems, staffing problems, vendor relationship problems, and quality assurance problems, to name only the most urgent. Harv's past experience and history of accomplishment show evidence of success with all of these except staffing. His ability to select capable individuals and develop them to meet organization requirements may be above average, but he has done very little of either and there is no information as to how successfully he did it or how much help he had. Moreover, since the last time he hired anyone, the manpower market has tightened up considerably.

This leads Manager X to look at the rest of the situation. Competition for reliable vendors has been increasing rapidly, so that there's a real challenge for Harv Langley here. Then, too, the firm's methods of operation, its policies, practices, and values, are all new to Harv. So are Manager X and the other associates with whom Harv is now working. To function effectively in this firm, and in the tightened manpower market, represents a whole series of development targets for Harv.

What about Harv himself? Why did he change jobs? What is he seeking in his new position? Why was he willing to accept the same sort of job at which he had already proved himself elsewhere? Since Manager X and Harv have already scheduled a trip to visit one of their major subcontractors, Manager X takes advantage of the time they have together to review this whole area. He learns that Harv left a much larger firm because he felt he was becoming too specialized. He sees his new affiliation as offering a more flexible career, hopes to go up the management ladder and broaden his scope of responsibilities. As a job hunter, he felt the greatest asset he had to offer a new employer was his past success in subcontract work, and he considers his continued performance in a similar capacity as his personal investment toward a broader future.

With this information, Manager X helps Harv set a development target. The explicit goal is for Harv to staff his organization within six to eight months with well-qualified individuals, at least half of whom will be promotable within three years. Manager X reasoned this way: There is a powerful development goal *implicit* in having to handle the work of subcontracting under different business conditions and in a new firm. This part of his job, then, probably doesn't need further reinforcement unless there are signs that Harv is not making the transition easily. There is no reason to believe he'll have any trouble; but, if he should, Manager X will have to see that he develops one or more appropriate goals in this area.

Harv wants broader responsibilities, however, and the selection and development of employees are critical to this ambition. So are other aspects of management, but this is one which Harv must tackle very quickly in order to make a success of his present job. Manager X therefore exploits this need, making only the one development goal explicit. This makes sense to Harv, who now will have an early opportunity to apply whatever knowledge and skill he has or can acquire.

Let's take another example—a longer-service employee this time. A financial specialist named *Larry Crawford* reports to Manager Y. Larry has an excellent education in economics which includes a master's degree in business administration. His early experience was in a variety of accounting functions, but for the past 14 years he has specialized in government contract administration. In fact, he is acknowledged to be one of the most knowledgeable men in the country in this field. He knows, of course, far more than Manager Y about his specialty.

Manager Y feels strongly that Larry is limiting himself by his continued specialization, but he realizes that the field is important and that the future is something for Larry to decide for himself. He does, however, want to fulfill his managerial responsibilities by making sure that Larry has sound career goals toward which he is working and that these are satisfying to Larry and of ultimate benefit to the company that employs them both.

As he reflects on the work Larry will be doing during the next six months or so, it does not appear to offer much stretch or challenge. Admittedly, Manager Y may be wrong—he simply is not familiar in depth with the field of government contract administration. Certainly Larry's small group is not likely to expand, since no change is anticipated in volume or kind of work needed —or in the environment or climate in which Larry will be working.

Manager Y realizes that a great deal depends on Larry's view of his job and his career. He therefore schedules a discussion during which Larry admits that he feels stale on the job but would like to continue specializing in government accounting because there are so few men in this important field. He hopes eventually for a higher-level staff position in the company, one in which he would be guiding and advising others doing the kind of work he is doing now. There is one big unknown. Larry is used to being personally responsible for the contract administration work. He doesn't know whether he would like a purely staff position.

Together Manager Y and Larry decide to add to Larry's present job some specific policy development for use by Manager Y's organization and for consideration by other government contract administrators in the firm. This will give Larry a taste of policy work and the opportunity to try to "sell" it to others who are not under his jurisdiction. It will also put into writing procedures which heretofore have existed only in Larry's mind. Privately, Manager Y resolves to supply Larry with as much information as he can about broad business plans and problems of financial management. He can use the regular staff meetings for the purpose and in this way, possibly, arouse Larry's interest. Manager Y also decides that he will hold group rather than individual progress review meetings to permit each employee to discuss his work in front of his associates, explaining where it stands, what's ahead, and what problems or obstacles he faces. The discussion and suggestions which are bound to follow should bring Larry more in tune with the total accounting work of the department. Depending on Larry's response to these measures, Manager Y will decide whether to encourage broadening or continued specialization. Finally, to help remedy his incomplete understanding of Larry's work, Manager Y decides to discuss with others in the firm the kind of improvements they believe are needed in contract administration and to invite at least one recognized specialist to spend a day or two with Larry and him—if necessary, going outside the company to find such an individual.

Notice what Manager Y has done. He has established new work goals for Larry—developing policy and influencing others in the company who do not report to him. And Manager Y has new climate goals for the man too—more general business information and more information in Larry's specialized field. Larry and Harv are only examples, of course. The decisions made by Manager X and Manager Y are intended only to illustrate how a manager weighs the possibilities available in the work, in the situation or climate, and in the individual himself and chooses what appear to be sound goals reflecting his consideration of all three. In real life, any number of equally effective goals might have been set.

How the Manager Gains Employee Acceptance

Fortunately, since the goals conceived by the manager concern the employee's development as well as the work of the department, there is no unilateral decision. The suggestions and ideas of the employee are a necessary ingredient of the goal-setting process. Certainly the manager needs the active help of the employee in attempting to explore the latter's career interests. And to insure reasonable success in achieving a goal—any goal—he needs the full cooperation of the employee. Moreover, if action taken by either manager or employee is likely to affect the employee's future, so that his stake in the outcome is high, there are ethical considerations involved. Not only must the employee understand the direction in which a goal might take him, but he must also, as we have seen, face whatever risks may be entailed.

Acceptance of development goals by the employee is, in fact, a critical point. Just as the manager has many demands on his attention, so the employee has a variety of work and personal goals competing for his effort. If the employee understands what is expected of him, but still his manager fails to get him to undertake certain development activities, whether for present or future work, surely it is because the employee either is not convinced of the goal's essentiality or puts it so far down on his priority scale that it rates little of his time and energy. Both employee and manager need the conviction that growth deserves a *high* priority.

What can a manager do, in actual fact, to gain employee acceptance of development goals and sustain employee interest in achieving them? Fortunately the "rules" are the same as for work goals and—to repeat a point made frequently in this book—may literally be work goals in which development is implicit.

1. Be sure the employee understands the importance of the goal to the firm and to himself, and involve him in formulating it.
2. Make the goal specific and measurable, and involve the employee in planning to meet it.
3. Provide early opportunity to apply learning and receive rapid feedback and appropriate recognition.
4. Renegotiate goals and plans as progress is made, and anticipate needed future efforts.

Be sure employee understands and is involved. The

typical employee will normally be more effective in doing his job if he sees how his work will be used and how it fits the organization's total plans. Similarly, he will normally try harder if he sees how his development efforts will add to his current and future contribution to meeting company goals and agrees this is desirable for him. One of the best ways of getting him to see this is to involve him in the collection of information which leads him to the conclusion that a certain goal *is* desirable.

For example, suppose the manager feels that Interviewer A needs to sharpen his interviewing skills so that he can make better predictions of probable performance on the job. He might suggest that Interviewer A make notes on a sample basis of what he believes, from his interviewing and reference-checking data, are each job candidate's performance strengths and weaknesses. After three or four months, he might then undertake a follow-up study with the managers who hired the recommended candidates to get their appraisal of the men's performance. Should Interviewer A, on comparing "before" and "after" data, find that the correlation between his recommendations and success on the job is low, he might well be asked to propose some steps he might take to improve his batting average.

Make goals specific and involve employee in planning. Motivation for most people increases when goals and plans are quite specific, are subject to measurement, and have due dates. Development goals have tended over the years to be a little vague and fuzzy; therefore, they have lacked the impact of the more measurable work goals. To make goals specific, however, sometimes requires quite a creative effort. If the employee, as well as the manager, is involved in this effort, the motivational impact is likely to be higher for both of them.

Suppose, for instance, that Employee Y needs to develop initiative. A target calling simply for "more initiative" is unlikely to produce any response from him but defensiveness and frustration. Instead, the manager should think ahead about what Employee Y will be doing during, say, the next month or six weeks and pinpoint what appear to him to be important opportunities for Y to *display* initiative. He might then sit down with Y, mention the occasions he has in mind, and ask Y to plan specific action for making the most of them. Manager and employee might do this together, or Y might prefer to go off and do it by himself, returning two or three days later with his plans. The manager in either case should be prepared to suggest alternatives and specific contributions he might make to reinforce Y's strategy.

Provide early application, feedback, and recognition. Development goals and plans need to be devised around opportunities that will occur *soon.* Adults forget rapidly. Something learned now, if not applied till next year, will probably have to be relearned. Feedback, whether from the manager, from the employee himself, or from other sources, must follow closely on action if it is to influence later action. Recognition is a great stimulant to continued improvement; however, during a learning period when the individual is unsure whether he is on the right track, it has special importance.

When Employee Y's manager calls his attention to coming occasions for displaying initiative, he chooses some that will occur within a month or six weeks. This gives Y time to think his plans through and put them into action while his target is still clear in his mind. If, after the first occasion, he and his manager sit down to review the effectiveness of the planned action, Y has the opportunity to adjust his plans for the next time. And if, during this discussion, the manager underscores what he thinks worked well and makes it plain that he is generally pleased with *Y*'s efforts (even though there is still room for improvement), this will encourage *Y* to try again.

Renegotiate goals and plans. Nothing is so dead as last quarter's plan which no longer fits this quarter's needs. As the manager sees the employee making progress toward development goals, he needs to work with the employee to update the agreed-on plans, taking that progress into account. In this way the employee is always working on current opportunities, always looking ahead, always trying to anticipate and prevent problems rather than solving them after the fact. Moreover, the process of revision helps sustain interest on both sides.

Constructive interaction—that is, information exchange, reinforcement, and renegotiation—all these serve to increase mutual commitment.

USING WORK TO
STIMULATE DEVELOPMENT

W<small>E LEARN BEST BY DOING. THE STATEMENT IS ALMOST A</small> cliché—probably every supervisor or manager agrees with it. But, having said it, it's hard to know what to do about it. Let's examine this old maxim in an effort to understand its implications for managerial action.

First of all, since all employees are doing something in their work, is learning inevitable? Granted a normal adult, the answer is yes. But *how much* learning occurs and *what* is learned are the issues. If an employee does the same thing day after day, learning falls off rapidly. Depending on his personal interest, he may see better ways to do things, he may find short cuts, he may even reflect on his latest reading while he performs his repetitive task, but the likelihood of very much work-related learning occurring after a certain point is small. For work to make a major contribution to learning, it needs to challenge an individual's existing knowledge and skill and require him to add to them. Even then what is learned may not be useful to the business. For this reason, the establishment of learning goals aimed at business needs is critical.

A clearly stated goal determines not only what work is done but where the emphasis is placed as well. For example, consider the work of an interviewer in an employment office. If personal development has not been factored into his goals and the company needs 12 technicians, he will set out to hire 12 qualified technicians. He will go through the usual process of advertising, interviewing, record keeping, interview arranging, and offer making. The first few times he does this he will learn quite a bit. After that, learning will begin to fall off. If he and his manager now revise his goal to one of not only hiring qualified technicians but making more accurate predictions of their on-the-job performance, the interviewer will probably work to improve the information he gets from former employers and will seek ways to improve his interviewing. In addition, he will probably take greater care to document his findings about job candidates and the basis for his predictions. His opportunities for certain kinds of learning are obviously much increased by this developmental focus in the revised goal.

If, on the other hand, the goal established for the interviewer is to improve the company "image" among the applicants and at the same time reduce recruiting costs, his efforts will assume a different direction. He will consciously work at the impression he makes and the information about the company he gives, and he will look for lower-cost ways of bringing applicants to the employment office. Clearly there is a hazard here. If costs are reduced at the expense of quality of employees hired or if, in his efforts to make a good impression, the interviewer fails to do a sound job of identifying the probable assets and liabilities of the candidates, there is a net loss to the firm. The development implications of the work goal must therefore represent a plus, an extra, an achievement beyond the normal results required from the work. In any event the importance of the goal in channeling development toward needed business and learning results is clear.

And the goal is important for another reason. If an employee and his manager agree on one as being within the employee's capacity to achieve in a reasonable period of time, the goal itself may be all that is needed to stimulate development. This assumes that no strong negative factors are present, of course. Many employees, having accepted a work goal with development implications, become so interested in achieving it that, on their own, they seek out whatever information they need, proceed to apply it, make any adjustments that seem necessary, and feel sufficiently rewarded by successful accomplishment that the manager has very little more to do.

Unfortunately, however, not all employees respond in this way—or perhaps it is more exact to say that conditions are not always such that even the best employees are able or willing to respond so satisfactorily. Assignments vie for attention, and for one reason or another development may be given a low priority. Once development goals have been selected, managers therefore need to learn a variety of ways to help the employee reach them, and one of the best is to use the work itself as a stimulant to growth. To do this, the modern manager needs to have a clear picture of the tools available to him.

What are some of the more powerful tools both for incorporating development experience into work goals and for making the doing of work more likely to produce growth?

Putting Development into Work

There was a time in management thinking when it was assumed that at each successive level in the organization most of the work was delegated to the next lower level and so on down the line. With today's increased professionalism and specialization of knowledge, that idea is no longer generally acceptable; work is seen to be quite different at different levels. The manager of a group of engineers designing a product is accountable for the design which finally comes from his organization, but he is not expected to do the design work or even, in many cases, to be able to do it. He is expected to staff positions with qualified engineers and organize the work so that successful design results from and, indeed, is facilitated by his efforts. It is his managing that he contributes to the design as his part in the overall work of the organization. This is an important distinction to make in thinking about development, because it gives the manager more flexibility in using his time and greater opportunity to be innovative in establishing and upgrading employee contribution levels. The starting point for his developmental action is the way he packages the work for each position.

Position design. This is the key to the most fundamental kind of work-based development. The position the employee holds represents, after all, his primary occupational commitment. Anything asked of him beyond his job is extra, often demanding some effort on the manager's part to insure agreement. But an employee's initial acceptance of the job and his continuance in it constitute in a very real sense a contract to perform the content of the job. This may require stretch, challenge, and much learning, or it may ask very little of the employee. The effect on his growth, as far as improved capacity to contribute is concerned, varies correspondingly.

By position design we mean the deliberate grouping of work responsibilities and work goals into a package to be performed by one employee, keeping in mind required relationships with other positions both inside and outside the organization. The manager must do two things if position design is to help in meeting the goals of the department and to offer development opportunities to employees. First, he must describe the position in terms of the end contribution it is to make to the business, not merely the immediate tasks or duties to be carried out. This gives the incumbent maximum opportunity to participate in formulating ways of carrying out the mission and to evolve approaches which will use his strengths fully. It also gives the manager the opportunity to build learning experiences into the position consistent with pressures for results and the employee's anticipated growth.

Second, the manager must keep each position in his organization dynamic by reviewing it frequently so that, as business needs, situational factors, and employee ability to contribute change, the position's content is correspondingly altered, consistent with whatever economic factors may be involved. He cannot, for instance, continue to increase the value of all jobs reporting to him indefinitely; that would put the price of work in his department out of competitive range. But he can balance out investments of this sort against contributions of increasingly greater value. The question is whether he is getting the firm's money's worth in his effort to add growth possibilities to the employee's job.

Rotating assignments. A manager shouldn't keep a productive, growing employee in a given job or allow him to remain in it for too long. Even though responsibilities and specific work goals may change with time, there comes a point when an employee's growth in a particular job slows down or evens off. The manager who wants to continue a high rate of development and perhaps even increase it may try to find a promotion for an employee. The employee may not be ready for promotion, or the available openings may not be suitable for him. It is often possible, however, to move him to a different job at his same salary or organization level, thus increasing opportunities to learn and broaden his experience. This plan does, of course, entail some risk and lack of economy. The employee needs to be willing to undertake the new work even though it may require a much higher initial level of effort on his part for the same compensation. He must have the basic ability to learn it within a reasonable time period. And the manager must be willing to invest the probable lower productivity in the hope of a higher contribution later.

There is some evidence that "lateral" transfer is not used often enough, that the risks are more frequently than not outweighed by an almost immediate upsurge of interest and effort on the part of the employee, and, in fact, improved results.

When the transfer process is repeated several times, the individual is said to be "on rotating assignment." For this device to be successful, the individual must feel he has actually changed jobs on a permanent basis and is expected to produce at least as much as the previous incumbent. If he feels that rotation is a gimmick, that he is just an observer or is merely "passing through" the assignment, the incentive for growth may not be there. This means the manager never for a moment expects less of an employee who is filling a job for so-called development reasons than he expects of one hired especially for the work. In fact, he may legitimately expect more.

Moreover, the new assignment should be carefully selected to fill a development gap. That is, it must actually represent new work or a different emphasis. The employee is assigned the job for what he doesn't know rather than what he is well qualified to do. Needless to say, the greater the discrepancy between his qualifications and the work requirements, the greater are the development opportunities. So, also, is the risk. Managers should therefore learn to pick assignments which represent moderate but not great differences in comparison with past experience. Success is then more likely, and both man and manager will be encouraged to continue their development efforts.

Finally, it is vital, when using rotating assignments as a development approach, to be sure the employee remains on each new assignment, in turn, long enough to get an accurate sample of the job's requirements and long enough to experience the results of his own decisions. There is no rule of thumb about the exact time. It will certainly vary with the complexity of the job, its organization level, and the importance of the relationships and contacts inherent in getting the work done. In less complex jobs, six months may be adequate. At the foreman level, a year may be required. At the superintendent level, two years or even more may be desirable.

A manager can help to make it easier to move from one position to another within the organization if he does a great deal of his work planning and reviewing on a group basis. When employees have the opportunity to describe in the presence of their associates how they plan to contribute to the department's results, the reasons why they have selected certain courses of action, the obstacles they are encountering and how they plan to overcome them, each gets a feeling for the other's work, becomes familiar with its peculiar problems, and finds the transition easier should he be asked to take on another job in the same organization.

Work plans and development plans. Rotating assignments can be expensive for the organization and may not be suitable for all employees. However, important development opportunities can be built into current work within the framework of the already established position. One of the easiest times to do this is during the process of establishing and updating individual work plans to meet needed business goals. The manager makes clear the commitments of his total organization; and the employee, on the basis of his position responsibilities as he understands them, suggests specific

---

Three Criteria for Success of Rotating Assignments

Rotating assignments are most likely to contribute to development if

1. Standards of accomplishment are at least as high as for a "permanent" assignee.

2. Assignment fills a development need of the employee.

3. Assignment is long enough to provide a representative sample of the work and the employee lives with the results of some of his important decisions.

measurable steps he feels he can take in order to contribute more fully to overall results. Together the two review these proposals until agreement is reached.

It is during this discussion that the development-minded manager considers not only whether immediate business demands will be met but also whether the work that is being planned requires the employee to acquire desirable new knowledge and skill. On the one hand, the manager can make certain that some of the work is new, that it is being done in a different way, that results are expected earlier than in the past, or that a new application of skill or knowledge is involved. Alternatively, he can insert into the work plan an improvement goal (a better way of doing recurring work, a new method or process) or an identified development goal (a needed performance improvement, a skill upgrading). For example, a manager who wishes a manufacturing engineer to improve his contact skills might focus on the goal of "simplification of the XYZ product design to cut manufacturing time by 30 percent." He might therefore suggest to the employee that, instead of doing the redesign himself, he put together a study team consisting of a design engineer, a foreman, a purchasing agent, and an inspector and secure the desired simplification through the combined thinking of this team. That would be a work-improvement goal implying development of a specific kind. To cite an example of a development goal as such, he might ask the employee to "improve his working relationships with the inspection organization and factory supervision so that manufacturing time on Product XYZ can be reduced by 30 percent." If the employee agrees, he develops specific steps he can take to bring about the improved working relationships.

In either case, when the manager reviews work prog-

ress, he emphasizes results in the contact area as well
as in time reduction, so that the employee sees the
priority the manager places on development and works
just as hard at skill improvement as at other aspects
of his job. In the first case development, of course, is
implicit. In the second it is stated explicitly. Depending on the employee, the emphasis the manager wishes
to give the development, and the relationship between
the two men, one method might take preference over
the other.

Special assignments, study teams, and task forces.
Sometimes certain kinds of growth do not lend themselves readily to achievement within the context of the
current position, yet the manager wishes a particular
employee or group of employees to have a certain kind
of work experience. He may feel he cannot afford rota-
tional assignments or that the potential gain is not worth
such a big step. In this case the so-called special assignment is a much-used device. The employee is asked to
do a piece of work which needs doing but does not
wholly belong within his responsibilities. He may be
expected to do the work by himself or to join a group
of employees similarly assigned to contribute their share
to its accomplishment. Such a group is often called a
committee, a task force, a study team. It is a temporary
group formed, usually, for a single work purpose.

The manager bent on development selects such special assignments and asks individuals to undertake them
with an eye not only to business needs but to employee
growth as well. The goal to be accomplished, or the
manner in which it needs to be accomplished, should
require the employee to add to his knowledge and skill
in ways which take him in the direction of identified
development goals. Extra value can be gained by care-

ful selection of the other members of the group, so that the employee can learn from them as well as from the work assignment.

Reinforcing On-the-Job Development

Compared to the stimulation which comes from doing challenging work, the manager's attempts to contribute to learning through coaching and other forms of interaction are much less consistently productive. It is certainly true that, for learning to occur, an individual must have not only the opportunity to apply what he has learned but also information as to his success in applying it, so that he can adjust his actions accordingly. Normally an employee relies on his manager for this information. How willing, then, is the manager to give it? Has his own experience made it possible for him to do so? How good are his teaching skills? Does his personality make it easy for him to give the employee counsel—and easy for the employee to take it? Does the employee accept the manager's experience as legitimate and relevant? Does he respect the manager's knowledge of the subject? What basic relationship exists between the two of them and with other members of the organization? Many of these questions will be discussed in some detail as we look at the impact of the manager's style on employee development. For the present, however, we shall limit our consideration to what the manager can do to make work an even greater developmental experience.

Day-to-day coaching. This development tool is most useful when the manager has specific knowledge and experience which the employee needs for his work or when the manager sees better ways for the employee to go about that work. The expectation is that, if he will merely transmit this information to the employee— coach him—the employee will be able to improve his performance and will have grown in the process. While this may hold true for the simple jobs, for beginning or junior employees, or for cases in which the manager is greatly respected for his unusual knowledge, attempts at coaching occasionally run into difficulty with more experienced employees, especially professional workers.

Here are some of the more important do's and don'ts for making coaching as effective as possible:

1. Keep the discussion brief, informal, and focused on the work as much as possible. Brief, because lengthy recitals of personal experiences may seem boring and repetitive to others. (The employee can be encouraged to ask questions freely.) Informal, because there is something about the private-office, solemn-tone-of-voice session which discourages the warm, constructive give-and-take which is likely to get results. A light tone of voice and a quip or two made in the work area are more conducive to employee acceptance. Focus on the work, because it is this in which you both have a legitimate stake. Only if the employee's behavior is affecting his ability to get results should it be discussed, and then in terms of specific instances and suggestions for improvement.

2. Make coaching positive and specific in content, constructive, and limited to one or two points at most which require change or improvement. Positive and specific, because from a communication point of view this gives the best chance for clear understanding. Constructive, so that some

useful help is given. Limited to one or two points, so that any natural defensive reaction on the part of the employee to criticism of what he is doing is minimized and his attention is focused on something of real importance which he can concentrate on correcting.

3. Structure the coaching session as a two-way discussion, an interaction. This improves the probability of adequate communication greatly, recognizes the importance of the employee's own knowledge and experience, minimizes defensiveness on both sides, and increases involvement and commitment.

4. Don't coach too much. Be selective in what you discuss and discuss it so that what you say is more likely to be welcomed by the employee. He needs the opportunity to think problems through, to make choices and decisions on his own. A more or less continuous critique of his work fails to emphasize what's important, minimizes his seeing things for himself, and may make him so dependent on you that he becomes fearful of moving ahead without your help.

5. Time your coaching carefully. Try to anticipate decisions or actions and, if coaching seems desirable, do it in advance. Nothing is more annoying than the manager who always knows a better way after the fact.

Information exchanges. For the mature, seasoned employee, the best replacement for old-fashioned coaching is the concept that useful information resides in both man and manager. The manager's perspective on the business, his information about the company's plans, his knowledge of how other organizations doing related work are progressing, his observations of the employee on the job—all these permit him to make a distinctive contribution to the employee's ability to grow through work. The employee, on the other hand, encounters and surmounts obstacles continually. He sees the improvement to be gained from different allocations of resources or courses of action. He may anticipate technical breakthroughs or identify unusual opportunities to benefit the whole organization.

When these two share their learning and adjust their ideas and actions accordingly, each is better able to do his job and development increases dramatically. Information need not be exchanged on a formal basis. There are no forms for the purpose. Yet the manager must

Organizing Development Tools
I. *Around Work*

Development Goals	
	Influence
Putting Development into Work	Position Design Rotating Assignments Work and Development Plans Special Assignments, Study Team, Task Force, Committee
Reinforcing On-the-Job Development	Day-to-Day Coaching Information Exchange Work Reviews, Business Reviews, Progress Reviews, Accomplishment Reviews Performance Appraisal Feedback Self-Feedback, Objective Standards

make deliberate plans for such exchange and encourage employees' participation not only with him but with each other as well.

Work reviews. These may be variously called work reviews, business reviews, progress reviews, accomplishment reviews. Essentially they require the manager, at specified points in time, to review assigned work on a somewhat formal basis. This doesn't mean that the meeting itself is formal; it merely means that the date and purpose of the meeting are specified ahead of time, both parties prepare for it, notes are kept during the session of decisions made, and from it emerge ideas and data which result in the realignment or redefinition of work and the updating of plans. It is an excellent occasion for the information exchange just described.

The development-minded manager uses such a session, not only to understand more fully where work stands with respect to commitments, but also as an opportunity to share information and personal experiences to whatever extent they seem to apply. It further gives him an occasion to determine how the employee's planned development is progressing. Is he indeed benefiting from new experience? Is he acquiring desirable information? Are his skills improving? Are his attitudes and interests shifting in desirable directions? The manager deliberately asks questions which permit the employee to display new knowledge, elaborate on parts of the work which require new skills. And, of course, he seizes the chance to build into the work ahead additional goals requiring employee development.

Most managers feel that about once a quarter is right for the progress review—or, better still, just before major milestones in the work are reached. Sessions need not be individual. A manager may hold them with all the employees who report to him or with groups of employees assigned to a project or doing related work. This is one of the great advantages of work-based development effort. Its focus is on work; its language is work; except for the intentions of the manager and the employee, it *is* work. And so there is much less need for private, individual discussion.

Performance appraisal feedback. Most companies ask the manager to discuss his appraisal findings with the employee. Many feel, however, that such a discussion does little to stimulate the employee's development. It is true that if the appraisal discussion gives him no new information (or fails to review forgotten or ignored information), and if it is not translated into its implications for future work and personal plans for growth, there is little likelihood of its having a developmental effect. Moreover, growth is not likely if the manager cites too many needed improvements at one time, so that the

---

Do's and Don'ts for Performance Appraisal Feedback

Performance appraisal feedback is most likely to have a useful development effect if

1. It gives the employee useful new information.

2. It is translated into future goals and action plans to reach them.

3. Criticism is given in small doses.

4. Reward and recognition seem to match contribution.

5. Discussion is work-focused.

6. Information is specific and constructive.

7. There is a two-way exchange of information.

employee becomes defensive, or if the appraisal is linked with salary recommendations and the employee feels the reward does not match the required effort. But, when the suggestions offered for day-to-day coaching are applied to this session, and when it is treated more like an information exchange, the resulting inter-action can contribute to changed attitudes on both sides, more acceptable employee development goals, a better perspective on needed improvements, and additional opportunities for the employee to apply new knowledge and skill.

Performance appraisal feedback probably is a better tool for setting development goals than for achieving them, but it can be used for both purposes.

Self-feedback. The things we learn for ourselves we usually absorb more readily and understand better than information that is given us by others. The manager who wishes to make work a developmental experience strives to reach agreement with the employee on the way in which success in the job will be measured. This is possible when the results to be achieved are stated in specific, measurable terms and when the criteria evolved are objective and, preferably, numerical. The employee is then able at all times to see where he stands with respect to needed results and can adjust his actions accordingly. Moreover, both man and manager are usually in agreement on work progress to date.

The marksman, attempting to improve his aim, has a much better chance when he sees where his bullet lodges in the target. Just so the employee, trying to improve his component design ability, learns rapidly when his design is incorporated in the product and he is able to see it function or at least find out how well it meets specifications. Not all work lends itself readily to this kind of objective feedback, but to the extent that it can be built into the work plan it is a powerful development tool.

Capitalizing on work represents the major opportunity for the manager to encourage employee growth. The job content is within his jurisdiction. There is a good choice of tools, important and powerful, almost all of which are within the ability of the typical manager to use effectively. Moreover, the employee himself, with no encouragement from his manager, can apply basic development concepts to his work and thus advance his career.

CHAPTER VIII

CREATING A
DEVELOPMENT CLIMATE

CHALLENGING WORK IS ESSENTIAL TO OCCUPATIONAL growth. Sometimes it is all that is required. But usually, as we have noted, the rate of growth is affected considerably by the setting or climate in which the work is done. The oversupervised employee, the employee who is never permitted to make even the smallest mistake without penalty, the employee who has minimum information about how his work relates to that of others, suffers in two ways: His growth is retarded, and his contribution to the business is impaired. Both factors in turn, of course, limit the effectiveness of the department in which he works.

A "development" climate is often thought to be a "soft" climate, a climate in which there is considerable freedom to do as one likes with little risk of penalty for nonperformance. The manager of such a laissez-faire organization is frequently pictured as being somewhat fatherly, certainly benevolent. This is sheer nonsense. Growth does not occur without vigorous, goal-directed effort, enormous self-discipline, heartbreaking trial and error and retrial. The growth of an individual within an organization, moreover, implies additional constraints so as not to hamper the development of his associates or decrease the likelihood of the organization's attaining its goals. This means a "tough" climate. There is considerable freedom, to be sure, but the demands for increased contribution are constant and yesterday's results are never good enough for today. The manager's personality is minor in its impact compared with his persistent expectation of self-set standards of excellence and self-measured results.

The development-minded manager who is determined to close the gap between actual and budgeted performance realizes this means creating and maintaining a work environment which not only permits but requires every employee to use and add to his abilities. In a sense, the creation of this climate is one of the manager's personal development goals, and he must plan carefully to meet it.

Climate—to repeat—is composed of many factors. The manager is the originator of some and the interpreter and integrator of them all. What he feels, believes, says, and does affects the employees' understanding of climate and their reaction to it. His influence, then, can be discussed under three headings: (1) the manager's personal work, (2) his interaction with employees doing their work, and (3) his specific attitudes about employee development. The action he takes in all three areas is colored and made more or less effective by his managing style.

The Manager's Work

The most fundamental part of the manager's job—and, it is to be hoped, the largest consumer of his time—is the part devoted to *managing*, to meeting his group's commitments. In addition, however, he has administrative duties—budget preparation, report writing, the presentation of new ideas—and a contribution to make to the work of the next higher level in the organization. Probably he also undertakes some personal work with customers, associates, and the like. He has numerous opportunities for stimulating employee development while carrying out all these responsibilities.

Personal example. While the content of their respective jobs may vary considerably, it is usually true that a large number of responsibilities are common to both individual worker and manager. For example, each explains and defends his work. Each makes plans which need to be sold vertically and horizontally. Each must operate within a budget. Each communicates both orally and in writing.

Particularly in the early years of an employee's career, the way his supervisor or manager carries on these normal activities becomes a model. The model may be either positive or negative; that is, the employee may try to do as he sees his manager doing, or he may deliberately try to be different because he sees or feels the deficiencies in his manager's performance. Even those activities which the employee may not currently share are observed—the manager's ways of handling them are very likely to be logged mentally for future reference. Later, when the occasion arises, the employee recalls what he has learned from previous managers and his actions are influenced accordingly.

In addition to the work they have in common, the manager's managing functions give him an opportunity to demonstrate the importance of employee development. When he reviews his organization structure, for example, he can discuss the development implications of proposed changes along with possible improvements in the flow of the work. Will the new organization capitalize on needed short-supply talent? Will it help put decision making where it belongs, or will it force the manager himself to make too many decisions, thus damping employee responsibility and learning? Will it provide knowledgeable senior specialists with an opportunity to share their experiences with newer employees?

When it comes to staffing, filling vacancies or newly established positions, the manager can balance the potential contribution to the company against the immediate qualifications of candidates. He can consider their probable future growth along with their ability to meet immediate goals. He shouldn't ask: "Will this man fit in?" Instead, he should put his question differently: "Will this man add to our learning experience so that we are all able to do our work better?"

Organization and staffing, needless to say, are only two examples. The manager's actions should show employees how to factor development considerations into all normal work, managing included.

Visibility of manager's work. The manager in fact should make his total job—the problems he is facing, the information he is gathering, the alternatives he is weighing, the decisions he is making—visible to employees. Thus he shares his personal learning experiences on the job in a very meaningful way and helps the employees understand what is expected of him. The employees are therefore better able to determine for themselves their interest in aiming at his or a similar job. They realize what they must learn to do and grasp, to some extent, the conditions that exist at the next higher organization level. And, since they see the context within which their own work needs to be done, they do it better.

Employees, moreover, see not only what the boss does and how he goes about doing it but his attitude toward it as well. If he is annoyed and disgruntled when certain requests are made of him, they quickly learn to relegate such requests to the bottom of the priority list. Does this mean the manager should show no emotion about his work, give no clue to his relative weighting of requirements? Of course not. His attitude is on display, though, and the greater the sense of commitment and enthusiasm he is able to generate for his personal high-priority work, the greater will be the sense of urgency he communicates. And the better he balances the individual demands made on him in terms of their importance to the total work of the organization, the better the employees will utilize their own time and effort.

Employee involvement. What all this amounts to is that the development-minded manager involves employees appropriately in the management of the department. He gives them a perspective on overall business needs, market opportunities, and customer requirements; he asks them to contribute information and ideas for use in planning. He involves them in the objective collection of data which will indicate how successfully they are meeting their commitments. He involves them in replanning when the original course of action does not meet with complete success, so that each employee learns from experience to face facts early and take corrective action.

This involvement in the management of the department is not at the expense of individual work. Rather, it helps make individual work more effective and satisfying since everyone understands better the reasons for the work and the way it fits into the total picture. Moreover, the planning and problem-solving skills developed as a result of active exposure to the manager's work are directly applicable to the employee's own job.

Like most good resolutions, the manager's determination to involve the employees in his work may fall by the wayside unless he takes planned steps to make involvement a reality. Fortunately, there are a number of ways in which the odds can be improved. Probably the best known and most frequently used methods are (1) debate, (2) playing the devil's advocate, and (3) summit meetings.

For example, when major decisions entailing heavy investment of money or time are to be made, a *debate* may be desirable. It is especially useful when the possible courses of action involve some unknowns and, therefore, the relative risks must be considered. The manager asks employees, individually or in a group, to defend the several alternatives, collecting data, preparing their respective cases, and presenting the most convincing evidence available to the manager, a group of peers, or some other selected audience. This is a powerful device for getting the pros and cons out on the table for all to see. It has the added advantage of being a sound development tool. Participating employees become absorbed in the details of preparation and presentation and add to their information as well as their persuasive skills. Even those who only listen hear the merits and drawbacks of each alternative and, when the decision is finally made, understand the basis for it.

Playing the *devil's advocate* is perhaps a form of debate. It is used primarily when one proposed course of action is favored. The manager, however, wishes to be sure that in selecting this particular alternative some major negative factors have not been overlooked. He therefore appoints an employee or a team to take the role of the opposition—that is, to collect evidence and develop arguments which might discredit the proposal. Those in favor, of course, try to counter the criticism. This, again, is a powerful aid to making difficult decisions as well as bringing employees into the decision-making process for their own benefit.

Summit meetings, business reviews, planning conferences, and the like are frequently used by managers and supervisors. Faced with having to plan for next year, develop strategy to counter a competitor's unexpected move, devise an advertising campaign, or choose among several possible investments, they call together the key individuals concerned. The group seldom conforms to strictly organizational lines—the amount of information or help a person can be expected to contribute is the criterion for admittance. Depending on the complexity of the situation, the members may go away for a few days or merely lock themselves into a convenient conference room. The point is that they divest themselves of all other demands on their attention until a course of action is decided upon. For the best results, such meetings should be scheduled well in advance, the topic or problem should be clearly defined, each individual should be assigned a task or an area for investigation, and the exposition part of the agenda should be well developed. The discussion which follows may be less formal, although most managers feel that the key questions to be answered or the major goals to be achieved should at least be listed. Once again, this sort of meeting serves both management and development interests.

It may appear at first glance that tools like the debate or the planning conference are useful only with employees of professional or supervisory status. This is not the case. As long as the subject matter is relevant to the work of the participants and the information they need to arrive at a sound decision is available to them, these types of meetings are just as useful with factory or clerical employees. For example, a debate by secretaries on the advantages and disadvantages of paying a girl on the basis of her boss's job in the organization may help clerical employees to understand the problems on both sides of this thorny question.

There are, moreover, obvious advantages to such

meetings. They offer the manager substantial assistance in getting his work done effectively. They require little specialized knowledge or skill on his part; he himself has probably participated in many of them, so that he is familiar with them even though he may never have thought of them as being developmental. He may, of course, delegate much of the preparation and detail to a staff man or other employee who will benefit from the experience. The major skill the manager needs is that of encouraging free discussion in very positive ways. The reasons for conflict and controversy need to be aired so that agreement is possible or, at least, the basis for favoring one decision over another is clear.

The manager may provide this encouragement simply by telling the group he wants free discussion. Better, he can demonstrate his willingness to listen to arguments pro and con by his reception of disagreement when it occurs. For example, after hearing Joe argue with Phil about the probable manufacturing cost of a new product line, the manager may say something like this: "Joe, excellent! We need more digging below the surface so we're not misled by appearances. Let's put a few figures on the board." Or: "I'm delighted there are at least two points of view here. Does anyone else see something we ought to consider?" In other words, he asks for wide-open discussion and shows how highly he values it when he gets it.

Interaction with Employees

Each employee does work which ties in with the overall commitments of the department, and the manager's personal association with him in doing this work has an important effect on his development. Chapter VII

considered the manager's role in reinforcing the learning stimulated by the nature of the work. There are,
however, a number of additional opportunities in the
work situation to improve the climate for learning.

Clarification of responsibilities. Not only should an
employee be given enough responsibility, but the manager should make sure he understands it. Most managers underestimate what an employee is able to do. Consideration should be given to past performance, of
course, but stretching is important too. Responsibility
for major accomplishment clearly expressed in results
terms is an excellent development motivator when
accompanied by probing, questioning, and examination
of alternative ways of achieving the required results.
Seeing the dimensions of a problem and the framework
within which it must be solved reinforces an employee's understanding of what is expected of him.

Encouragement of risk taking. Learning comes from
doing new things. Risk is, therefore, inevitably a part of
development. The manager's role is to encourage the
employee to estimate risk factually and take it when it
appears reasonable. You don't learn to drive a car in
downtown traffic, but neither will you make much
progress as long as you confine your efforts to reading
the driver's manual. Helping to identify the point at
which the new driver should take the wheel is, in
effect, the manager's contribution to development. Most
of the time he is overcautious. The employee needs to
step out on his own, make some mistakes, learn for himself what he does well and not so well, and—above
all—determine *when* he needs help, from *whom*, and
how to get it.

Standards. The most important contribution a manager can make in this area is to help the employee set
standards of excellence for his work. But knowing what

is "excellent" under various conditions is not a simple matter. The employee must learn to consider what he is asked to do, estimate the time and other resources available to do it, and within this frame of reference discuss with his "customer" what he feels is the best he can do—whether this customer is another employee who will use his work or someone outside the firm. Their joint decision then becomes the standard for the work, although it may need the manager's approval if overall company goals are involved.

Managerial support. Psychologists frequently say that for an employee to develop, the manager's attitudes and behavior toward him should be "supportive." This word implies that he should be warm, helpful, and encouraging. Excellent as these qualities are, however, the strongest support a manager can give is to demonstrate that he *expects* the employee to achieve the desired results and is *sure* he will do it.

Information and communication. Since full information about the progress of the business, changes in company thinking or plans, and anything else that may affect the ability of the employee to make sound decisions and adjustments on the job provide the manager with one of the best development tools he has, he should organize a system of meetings, reviews, and other communication devices—oral and written, formal and informal—which will make the exchange of information an easy, normal part of working life. Accent should be on use of information for improved work, however, not just on the supply and receipt of information for its own sake.

Particularly important to the manager for improving his capacity to manage and to the employee for developing his objectivity and his analytical and planning skills is the ability to accept unfavorable information—

to study it reasonably and thoughtfully, emphasizing its importance in adjusting work plans. A manager's ability to make sound decisions is impaired if unfavorable information is hidden from him so that he must search for it actively or establish special organizations to help him get it. And the growth of employees who live in such a climate is stunted.

Reward and recognition. Obvious though it may sound, it can't be said too often that the difference between good and poor work must be recognized and success rewarded in both monetary and nonmonetary ways. Moreover, it is equally essential that the striving for improvement become so important within the organization that accomplishment generates internal satisfaction—that is, self-reward.

These are management principles which represent great development opportunities, but their generality works against them. A manager needs a powerful device to help him put them to use effectively. One of the most important of these devices is *negotiation* or *renegotiation.*

In his efforts to insure meeting the department's commitments, the manager determines the specific contribution of each employee and its probable timing. Telling the employee what this is—or even asking him to meet certain goals—may distribute the work, but its development impact is close to zero. Encouraging the employee to identify, defend, and sell the contribution he believes he can make (either individually or with his associates), together with the resources he will need to meet quality and timing specifications, takes a little longer but has greater payoff possibilities in the end. It invites negotiation between employee and manager and among the employees themselves. This active give-and-take demands that each employee gather information and analyze it in advance. It requires him to consider alternatives and to recognize and anticipate the problems and risks in various courses of action. Moreover, when agreement is finally reached among all concerned, the level of individual and group commitment is high.

Since, during the negotiation process, manager and employees challenge each other's assumptions and the accuracy of each other's information and conclusions, the final decision is likely to have both a rational or factual basis and an emotional one. It does, of course, place a greater burden on the manager. He must see that every employee has or is able to obtain enough information about the company's needs and the availability of resources to make an intelligent contribution. Nor is negotiation a one-time affair. As the work progresses and circumstances change, employee and manager must renegotiate, adapt to the changed situation. But, as with the other means of reinforcing employee learning by interaction, the benefits to be gained far outweigh the cost in managerial time and energy.

Specific Development Attitudes and Actions

Manager's personal development plan. A manager who expects employees to make extra efforts to develop their abilities must himself take such steps and make these steps visible. Herein lies a real danger, however. If his development efforts in any way give the impression that he is interested only in advancing himself, regardless of the good of the organization, he may lose employee confidence and destroy an otherwise favorable climate. His efforts, therefore, should be primarily directed toward improving his current performance so that its effect is linked with the success of the department.

Priority of development in manager's work. As we have said, development is a normal, major aspect of the effective manager's daily job. In any plans he has for his department or for personal accomplishment, employee development goals are listed along with other needed work, and his actions to meet those development goals are as carefully planned as other work products. Indeed, he sees development as needed *work.* This means allocating the necessary time and setting a priority on it commensurate with its importance. He considers such time and effort an investment, however, and demands a suitable level of return from this investment—a return which shows up in terms of improved business results.

Manager's expectations for employee development. The successful manager assumes that employees want to and will develop. He makes this assumption clear by negotiating a higher contribution from each employee whenever work plans are reviewed. He lets the employee know that what was good enough last time is not good enough now. He sees such a strong relationship between the growth of employees and business results that he is just as likely to ask for a development result as for a work result and to give it as high a share of his personal attention, interest, and follow-up.

Explicit employee development goals. When work plans are established for the organization or for individual employees, the manager makes certain that at least one of these goals is explicitly development-based —that is, it represents a significant improvement in doing work or a significant addition to knowledge and skill.

Reward system. The manager bases his rewards—his monetary and nonmonetary recognition system—on successful development efforts as well as work results because he feels that these are mutually supportive. He takes pains to let his own manager know how well employees are doing and makes sure they know they are receiving earned credit.

Measurement of business success. While measuring success, the manager looks at employee development as a business commitment and refuses to consider the business healthy unless there is evidence of substantial individual growth. He finds such evidence in employee data on promotions, length of time on current job, increased depth of technical knowledge, and improved business results traceable to improved employee know-how.

Managerial Style

Permeating the way a manager does his work, interacts with employees, and expresses and demonstrates his convictions about employee development is his style of managing.

Its impact on the climate for development is obvious. Not so obvious is the way in which a manager, even one who understands his style fairly well and sees its impact on various individuals or the organization as a whole, can either modify his behavior to effect a more favorable impact or help employees understand him better so that any unfavorable results are minimized.

Some perceptive managers almost automatically adjust their style when they move into a new position, when they begin reporting to a new man, or when they sense an unfavorable response from an employee, an associate, or a customer. Most managers, however, are not able to make substantial changes without help. Sometimes such help is available from the personnel department or from an outside professional counselor or consultant. Occasionally the manager's own manager is able to assist him. Unfortunately, the standard forms of training in human relations and psychology have not been effective enough, nor have individual reading and reflection on the subject provided the kind of personal insight many managers need to make significant changes in their managing styles.

Because of the serious nature of this problem, however, considerable attention has been given to it in recent years, and there are a growing number of tools available for the manager's use. *All require professional guidance.* All are based on the assumption that if an individual sees more clearly the effect of what he says and does on other people, he will be more able and more likely to take the needed adaptive steps. If, in addition, he feels free to experiment with different ways of working with others, to change his usual methods of behavior and get rapid, honest feedback on the effect of the changes, he will be in a still better position to make sound modifications in his style.

Laboratory training. This is a general term for a group method of learning through personal experience about one's ability to establish relationships, to work with other people. Edgar Schein[1] defines it as "an educational strategy which is based primarily on the experiences generated in various social encounters *by the learners themselves*, and which aims to influence attitudes and develop competencies toward learning about human interactions." The format and duration of the laboratory vary considerably depending on the sponsor, trainer, or consultant in charge. In general, however, a variety of

[1] See Schein, Edgar H., and Bennis, Warren G., *Personal and Organizational Change Through Group Methods: The Laboratory Approach,* John Wiley & Sons Inc., 1965.

training techniques is used, including presentation of information, problem solving, role playing, discussion, and the case method. Perhaps the most discussed technique is the small learning group called the T-group ("T" standing for "training").

The participants in the T-group are usually placed in an unstructured situation—no assigned goal to accomplish, no leader to direct them. In these unusual, uncomfortable circumstances, some individuals take action, try to organize, try to "get things going." The others react to them. Since all are encouraged to express themselves fully, the individual feedback which results provides a basis for changing behavior in an effort to change reaction.

At a later stage of the laboratory, T-groups may be given problems to solve. The members are encouraged not only to solve the problems but to examine their behavior while doing so. The role of the professional staff is that of supplying general information and structuring situations to provide learning experiences. Only seldom do they give direct counsel or advice to individual participants.

Laboratory training, then, provides a way for an individual to see himself as others see him when he is not under the pressure of trying to accomplish a work goal for which he is responsible. Theoretically at least, he is able to focus his entire attention on his behavior and his reaction to others' behavior and thus gain important insights about himself, especially as he relates to other people. He is free to experiment with behavioral changes, to see which ones improve his effectiveness and may therefore be used back on the job.

Sensitivity training. This term, often used synonymously with "laboratory training," more properly refers to the specific objective of some laboratories—that is, "sensitivity" to the reactions of others to oneself and of oneself to others.

Managerial grid.[2] The grid is a device for describing the extent of managerial emphasis on people and production. Its application permits the meaningful description of various kinds of managing styles and their likely impact on an organization. Used in conjunction with laboratory training, it helps shift the participants' focus from broad personal characteristics and the ability to establish all kinds of human relationships to the more specific characteristics and relationships of a manager in business or industry. The authors of *The Managerial Grid* provide a self-report quiz which is used before, during, and after the laboratory learning experience. It supplies feedback on changes in philosophy, values, and attitudes which may have occurred during the session. The use of such an instrument facilitates discussion and group interaction and helps center it on the subject of managing.

Leaderless group discussion. The technique of forming discussion groups which are relatively unstructured and for which no leader is appointed is not limited to full-scale laboratory training. It is used in business and industry, in social and community organizations. It requires a specially trained counselor, preferably a professional, to assist in setting the ground rules and creating the climate, provide some information, perhaps provide instruments to facilitate discussion, and help the group see itself functioning.

The catalyst. Some of the results of laboratory training are possible within the framework of a business or industrial organization through the use of a specially trained third party or catalyst. This is an individual who

[2] Blake, Robert R., and Jane S. Mouton, *The Managerial Grid*, Gulf Publishing Co., Houston, Texas, 1964.

Organizing Development Tools
II. Around Climate

Development Goals

Influence

Manager's Work	Personal Example
	  Work
	  Attitude
	Visibility of Manager's Work
	Employee Involvement
	  Debate
	  Devil's Advocate
	  Summit Meetings, Business
	    Reviews, Planning Con-
	    ferences

Interaction with
  Employees Doing Their
  Work
	Clarification of Responsibilities
	  Risk Taking, Standards,
	  Managerial Support, Informa-
	  tion, Reward
	  Negotiation

Specific Development
  Attitudes and Actions
	Manager's Personal Develop-
	  ment Plan
	Priority of Development in
	  Manager's Work
	Manager's Expectations for
	  Employee Development
	  Goals
	Reward System
	Measurement of Business
	  Success

Managerial Style	Insight, Change
	  Laboratory Training
	  Sensitivity Training
	  Managerial Grid
	  Leaderless Group Dis-
	    cussion
	  The Catalyst
	  Psycho-Drama, Socio-Drama

works with a manager or an organization to help solve work-output problems through improved understanding of the human issues involved. For example, the engineering organization may claim a product is not being made properly and, therefore, customers are complaining; whereas the manufacturing organization claims the product is so designed as to be impossible to make satisfactorily. Here is a situation on which the catalyst might well go to work. He might collect information by interview or questionnaire from key individuals on both sides. He might then get the respondents together and feed back his findings to them. He might even ask them to take part in a leaderless discussion during which he would help them examine their interaction. Out of the effort should come improved understanding of their common problems and the relationships they need to establish in order to solve them.

Psycho-drama or socio-drama. This is another method of group learning in which the participants act out their interpersonal problems, playing themselves to start but often switching roles later on. The objective is to clarify the problems through dramatization, to obtain the benefits of self-insight and the reactions and insights of others who may be participating in the dramatization or observing it. While the method was developed primarily to help solve personal problems, it is a useful business training device, particularly when skill improvement and attitudinal change are involved. For best results a trained counselor is needed.

In considering group methods of training, a frequent question is whether the group should be composed of individuals from a single organization or whether it should be made up of strangers. There are, unfortunately, advantages and disadvantages both ways. The hope of learning carryover to the work situation is perhaps greater when the group is from the same organization. On the other hand, there is less freedom to react and experiment with behavior when working relationships have already been established. In this case, learning may be lessened; moreover, sometimes antagonisms are built in the learning sessions which are difficult to overcome back at work. The issue, therefore, needs to be resolved in light of the total manager development plan for an individual, department, or company.

Relatively few companies provide the personnel and facilities needed for sound application of the group dynamic methods just described. Managers who wish help in making behavioral changes—changes in their managing style—must usually seek it from outside agencies. The business school or psychology department of a nearby college or university is probably the best source of information on the availability of group training. It is perhaps unnecessary to say that changing a manager's style is difficult and the available tools for doing it are far from perfect. Critical to success are the determination of the individual manager to understand himself and others better, his desire to receive and use information which will help him do this, and his willingness to experiment with his own behavior in an effort to learn to work with others more effectively.

Moreover, changing style—even in what appears to be a sound direction—doesn't always achieve the desired results. A manager may decide that his particular style is not getting the best results for the organization or for a particular individual in it. He may then deliberately vary his delegation, his expectations, his degree of employee involvement, his follow-up of assigned work, and so on, only to find that the change is viewed with suspicion and a "What's he up to now?" reaction.

Like all change, therefore, change in managing style

needs to be planned. It can be introduced gradually in a series of logical steps, or it can be explained in advance to pave the way for employee acceptance. In any event, it is important to avoid sudden *unexplained* change.

Those who preach the importance of managing style have sometimes been so enthusiastic about the development results that come from style modification that there has been a tendency to overestimate its effect. It is true that a manager whose style promotes self-development efforts, innovation in work methods, and accomplishment contributes heavily to employee growth. An effective managing style, however, is not sufficient for growth. There must be, in addition, the element of challenging work which requires a man to add to his knowledge and skill in important ways. And the work needs to be in harmony with his basic abilities and career interests for maximum effect.

CHAPTER IX

ENCOURAGING INTEREST
IN SELF-DEVELOPMENT

POWERFUL THOUGH HIS DEVELOPMENT TOOLS MAY BE, A manager's ability to give direction and acceleration to employee growth has important limitations. The work he is able to assign is dictated by the business he is in, by the overall plans and strategy of his company, and by the demands of his customers. The climate he sets is influenced by his personality as well as many other factors over which he lacks full control. Equally important is the fact that every employee responds to work and working conditions in a highly individual way and this response, in the last analysis, determines the kind and amount of growth which ultimately result for him.

John Jones, for example, operates in a competitive climate in which his scrap and rework are published in a weekly report along with those of other foremen. He resents this constant control and worries about it continually. Building his defenses in advance, so to speak, he invests considerable energy in documenting last-minute changes in instructions, faulty materials, delays, and so on. If he shows up poorly one week, he is ready with his explanation—at the expense of production. *Pete Smith*, on the other hand, is exhilarated by the competition; he goes about energetically looking for ways to reduce scrap and rework so that he and his department will head the weekly list.

It is important for managers to realize that such differences do exist and be able to recognize them. Either they must work with the individual to change his response, or they must regulate controllable factors so as to capitalize on those which have the most favorable effect.

A good manager does a great deal of this intuitively. His level of expectation is almost automatically lower for an inexperienced than for an experienced employee. Consciously or unconsciously, he modifies the design of the position to suit the individual. He puts into it certain responsibilities which he feels the individual is uniquely qualified to handle. When they negotiate a work plan, he keeps in mind the employee's abilities and interests—as, of course, the employee does for himself when he recommends work goals and ways of reaching them.

A skilled manager also adjusts the working climate in ways he may hardly recognize. If the employee works best on his own, with minimum supervision, the manager tends to give him considerable freedom and independence. If, on the other hand, the employee shows a desire to talk things over, to share working experiences, the manager finds himself making frequent opportunities for doing this.

This modification or adjustment of working conditions doesn't interfere with the work of getting needed results. Rather, the seasoned manager adapts his practices and behavior in a way which he believes will get the best performance from a given employee. It is his clear, though perhaps unstated, recognition of the differences which exist in people; and, by and large, it represents a sound technique for him. Moreover, failure to take the individual's unique qualities into consideration can nullify his efforts to make the work developmental or climate facilitating. For example, the manager may say: "*Sam Spivak* has been a vibration specialist for many years. This year let's expose him to a greater range of technical problems, so that he's working in new areas, has contact with different concepts, and can grow in a broader field." Sam, however, may have made up his mind to become more and more deeply involved in the vibration field, may like the national recognition he receives as a specialist without peer in a very narrow area. The manager's attempts to enlarge Sam's work may result in anxiety, disturbance, rebellion—any number of emotional reactions. In fact, the manager may be interfering seriously with Sam's continued development.

Now take *Joe Rossi*. Suppose that Joe is a service-minded individual, likes a "busy" job in which he's continually responding to the requests of other people. Perhaps he's a whiz at purchasing. Joe's manager may say to himself: "Joe has worked terribly hard these last four years. He really hasn't had much opportunity to look at the broader aspects of the business or to consider different ways to solve old problems. I think I'll put him on a six months' semi-research project. It needs to be done and should give Joe a real change of pace." It *will* give Joe a real change of pace. But it will have a favorable effect on Joe's growth only if he can respond to much more relaxed conditions and is willing to give the assignment a try.

Over and beyond such normal adjustments, however, managers make an important contribution to personal growth by expecting individuals—indeed, encouraging them in very positive ways—to work toward their own development. After all, employees' stake in the direction and rate of their growth is as high as the manager's, if not higher. Their values must determine the desirable balance between occupational growth and growth in family, community, and other areas. They must therefore share in the responsibility for the decisions which involve them in development efforts. They cannot accept a passive role, waiting, in effect, to be developed.

What are some of the specific approaches and tools available to a manager to help him encourage responsible, active employee commitment? To help him induce those individuals reporting to him to use their abilities fully, enlarge on them, and move in the direction of a satisfying, self-fulfilling career?

Identification of Career Goals

Every individual is responsible for the use or waste of his personal talents. This means knowing what they are and what kinds of activities will strengthen and mature them. In the past, a person was forced to discover this by trial and error. Today, improvements in testing and other diagnostic tools make short cuts possible.

Professional counseling. A manager should encourage his employees to seek professional advice about their careers in general and specific talents which they may have and which might benefit from increased application and additional training. Counseling is not a one-shot affair, done once and then translated into a life-long plan. Individual interests change, talents emerge, employment possibilities shift dramatically. Counseling information, therefore, should be updated periodically. Perhaps every five years might be a good schedule, at least in the early stages of a person's career.

The manager can be of concrete help in this area by

providing a list of responsible nearby counselors or agencies, a description of the kind of service provided, the fees charged, and similar information. The personnel department may of course supply this information and, in large companies, even offer a counseling service of its own. There is, however, considerable advantage in letting the individual work with an independent adviser whose interest is fully centered on his client.

The manager can also help by offering to explore with an employee any thoughts he may have for incorporating the findings and recommendations of career advisers into current work and improvement goals. No manager, obviously, should insist on knowing the full results of the counseling; this is the personal domain of the employee. But a sincere interest in helping to apply whatever information is volunteered has a decidedly reinforcing effect.

Self-analysis. Employees, naturally, can analyze their own abilities, interests, and values to a great extent. As they perform their day-to-day jobs or engage in other activities, it rapidly becomes apparent to them that certain tasks are easier or more enjoyable than others, that certain accomplishments bring greater self-satisfaction.

Deliberate reflection on what one has learned and what one does best and how this knowledge can be applied most usefully in the future is both a stimulant and a reinforcement to learning. A manager encourages constructive self-analysis of this sort when he explores the employee's reaction to his work and the lessons he has learned from it and, at the same time, looks at progress made toward meeting commitments and modifying work plans for the future. For example, if Manager T has just filled an open position in his organization, his manager can help him get maximum value from the experience by reviewing with him what he has learned about good manpower sources, how he feels about his interviewing skill, what he estimates the new employee's performance strengths and weaknesses are likely to be, what plans he has made to make the transition into the new position as smooth as possible, and what he would do differently the next time. Out of this discussion, which crystallizes Manager *T*'s thoughts about himself as a selector of employees, may emerge one or more selection improvement goals to be implemented before the next job opening occurs.

Employees also make choices—in position, in assignments, in work methods, in relationships—which reflect their personal value system. The more such values are brought into the open, examined, and understood, the better able the employee is to direct his career soundly. Schuyler Dean Hoslett says:

> Self-analysis as a bench mark for development comes to the forefront of our thinking even more impressively today than it might have . . . [earlier] in the light of recent developments emphasizing the very real possibilities of conflict between personal goals and values on the one hand and organizational goals on the other.[1]

This is not an area for intrusion by the manager; but, since he is a major source of information about the organization in which the employee is working, he therefore has an obligation to make clear its basic philosophy, strategy, and plans so that the employee can take account of them in his thinking.

Isn't there some danger that the employee who objectively faces the question of what he wants to make of his life may find that his decision is incompatible with

[1] Hoslett, Schuyler Dean, "Self-Analysis: Bench Mark for Development," *The Personnel Job in the 1960's*, AMA Management Report 63, 1961.

his current work or the direction in which his career
with the organization is likely to go? For example, may
not an individual who has a strong desire to advance
democracy in the world feel he cannot do so within a
given industrial framework? Yes, this can happen—but
he may instead find a product and service orientation
for his talents which satisfies his basic interests. Or his
thoughtful examination of his feelings may lead to selection of off-the-job activities which advance his ambitions. Regardless of whether his introspection and
decision lead him to leave the firm, transfer within it, or
adjust his personal goals so that they are compatible
with his work, the better alignment of work and fundamental interests which results will ultimately lead to
more wholehearted commitment to what he is doing.
If he fails to achieve this alignment, he will almost certainly have some reservations which will inevitably
mean less than adequate satisfaction and self-respect—
with the consequent impact on work performance.

Yes, there's a risk involved, as in all development
activity, but there is also the promise of commensurate
payoff. For the deliberate decision to accept the conditions of a job and continue in it brings greater likelihood of its contributing to personal growth than remaining in it through inertia.

Managerial feedback. The manager, in addition, is a
source of much information about the employee as seen
by others. When he passes along such information—
whether it is about job performance, outstanding talents,
or likely direction and rate of growth in the organization—he is supplying important data for the employee's
personal planning.

It must be recognized, further, that individuals tend
to pursue directions and methods to which they are
accustomed. When a manager wants to encourage an

employee to explore new fields and test new interests, he needs to structure choices fairly narrowly, though imaginatively, so as to avoid selection of the old stand-bys.

The manager's contribution here is one of not only sharing his judgments but also working with the employee, to whatever extent the employee will permit, to factor the feedback information into current work and behavior.

Computer feedback. There are intriguing possibilities for individual use of computer data to evaluate progress toward career goals on a more objective basis. It has been pointed out that if, in the years ahead, it is possible to identify the kinds of career paths or experiences which frequently lead to certain positions in an organization, the employee will be able to identify himself by code to the computer and, on the basis of his career to date, ask for an evaluation of the likelihood of achieving a specified job or jobs. He can also adjust career variables in an effort to determine what further experience would increase his chances of success. While a totally accurate appraisal of individual potential is—perhaps fortunately—impossible, he can realistically attempt to improve the odds in his favor.[2]

Knowledge and Skill Increased

The employee now has a basis for making and reviewing personal decisions about the direction and priority of career goals. Even the most realistic goals, however, require implementation for achievement. Usually the first step is to keep relevant knowledge and skill current and hope to advance and enlarge them.

[2] See Ferguson, Lawrence, "Better Management of Managers' Careers," *Harvard Business Review*, March-April 1966.

There is simply no substitute for knowledge. It is the foundation on which all personal growth and development are built. Yet it has been very popular for development experts to play down reading and course work as being significant contributors to individual growth. There are reasons for this downgrading, of course. In the absence of substantive development goals and plans, managers may suggest a book or a course. For example, the consistent recommendation that anyone and everyone take a course in public speaking is an old family joke to personnel specialists who scan appraisal forms in search of common employee needs. But the purposeful pursuit of knowledge which has application in one's work or one's total personal plans deserves an important place among development tools.

The key point is to see knowledge in its proper perspective. By itself, it may not represent individual growth. When it is goal-directed, personally assimilated and integrated, and then used so as to change one's values, behavior, or talents, *then* it becomes growth.

For the manager, the implications are these: As development goals are set for the individual or the organization, he should encourage the acquisition of any background material that may be necessary to meeting those goals and the use of every possible scrap of knowledge or experience available. He can do this through suggested reading, asking competent library personnel to help select materials. He can recommend course work, making use of in-house programs as well as those of outside institutions. He can plan short discussions at regularly scheduled meetings and ask individuals to make presentations. He can, more than anything else, take time to check with the employee to see that he is using the best and most up-to-date information as he goes about his work. In technical fields, managers seem to do this more or less automatically. In other specialized company functions, in management, and in human relations, such concern is less seldom seen and, perhaps, much more needed.

In recent years there have been a number of developments in education of which managers and employees should both be aware.

Programmed learning, teaching machines, and programmed texts.[3] These are teaching techniques by which the content of a course is divided into small segments for presentation to the student. He is then asked a directly related question to determine his understanding. If he answers it correctly, he is told so and moves on to the next segment. If he answers incorrectly, he is told why he is incorrect—after which he goes back, reviews the given information, and tries the question again until he chooses the correct answer. The terms *programmed learning* and *programmed instruction* apply to the overall technique. If the information is supplied by a machine and the student records his responses by means of the machine, it is called a *teaching machine*. If the method utilizes a textbook, it is called a *programmed text*.

There are obvious advantages to this way of presenting information. It applies well-established teaching principles so that learning is very likely to occur and is reinforced through immediate feedback. (Research studies show that learning does, in fact, take place.) It permits the student to progress at his own pace since it is an individual process—there's no waiting for others to catch up and no frustration due to inability to keep

---

[3] For more detail, see Lysaught, Jerome P., "Industrial Training Through Programmed Learning," *Personnel Journal*, September 1961; Blood, Jerome W., editor, *The Personnel Job in a Changing World*, AMA Management Report 80, 1964; Ofiesh, Gabriel D., *Programed Instruction: A Guide for Management*, American Management Association, 1965.

up with the class. For adults out of school a varying number of years, this is desirable. Programmed instruction does, however, require very careful advance preparation of course material; therefore, it is relatively difficult to introduce changes in content. A manager who suggests a programmed course to an employee needs to be sure that the content is relevant, current, and suited to the prospective student's level of sophistication.

Simulation, role playing, in-basket, and business games. It is obvious that the more nearly course material matches working-life conditions, the easier it should be for a student to make the necessary translation to his work. *Simulation* of real situations therefore has been a desirable classroom goal for some time and, with the advent of model building and computer technology, has become even more popular.

In skill-improvement programs, *role playing* is frequently the only way for an instructor to see how well his principles have been grasped and how able the student is to put them into practice. One person takes the role of a manager, for example; another, that of an employee; and together they practice pre-employment interviewing or appraisal feedback. An entire group may participate, or some of the members may serve as audience. Later discussion brings out suggestions for improvement.

The *in-basket* exercise or test already described (see Chapter V) has proved to be an excellent training device for classroom use. It may consist, for example, of materials representing a cross section of items which might find their way to the desk of, say, a foreman. The student shows how he would handle each item if it were his responsibility to do so. Members of the class may and often do describe different ways of handling the same item. From the discussion, principles of supervision or management are evolved in a way which seems more meaningful than the old lecture method.

In a *business game*, a typical business problem or situation is set up and, with or without the help of electro-mechanical devices, information is fed to students who work either individually or in teams. They make decisions to take certain action on the basis of this information, see the effect of their action rapidly absorbed into the system, and get back new information on which they base further action. And so the cycle is repeated. The net effect is to show students how to pinpoint a problem, analyze the factors affecting it, and anticipate the effect of their decisions. Compared with real life, the time span of the cycle is shortened considerably—which, of course, creates certain pressures but also adds to the opportunities for learning.

The *case study* is not new, but our understanding of how to use it to the student's advantage has increased a great deal in recent years. A somewhat disguised but detailed description of a problem that has arisen in a business or industrial situation is given to the student. He is asked to read the material, identify what seem to be the critical issues, clarify them, and—he hopes— solve the problem. During class, the case is discussed, each member presenting his views. There are seldom any simple "answers" to problems, particularly in the management area, but the variety of approaches and thoughts expressed gradually makes certain basic principles apparent.

The case method is especially suitable for mature individuals who bring considerable personal knowledge and experience to the discussion and are thus able to contribute to, as well as learn from, other viewpoints. To the extent that the student develops personal philosophies and guidelines, he is likely to apply them on the job.

All these teaching methods, as well as the older lecture and demonstration techniques, are useful when properly handled. The age-old problem, however, remains: Can the student make use of what he has learned back on the job? Most educators feel he can if the climate is right; that is, if the manager will reinforce the learning rather than negate it by his own actions and attitudes. When a manager, therefore, exposes an employee to any of these devices, he has the responsibility of finding out what learning is likely to occur so that he will be in a position to recognize and reward its successful application. It should be clear that if he and the employee are working toward the achievement of specific development goals, and if the training constitutes one step toward meeting them, the odds are improved that needed reinforcement will occur.

Participation in professional organizations. Technical societies, trade associations, and other professional groups can be useful in transmitting new knowledge and stimulating interest in it. Such organizations help the individual to stay abreast of his field, hear about important new developments, make firsthand contacts with outstanding members of his profession, and, of course, gain recognition from his associates for good work accomplished. In other words, active participation brings "fresh air" into an employee's professional life, permits him to look at his work from a different perspective and gain insights into different ways of approaching its problems.

Most managers recognize, however, that important results only occasionally come from attendance at professional gatherings. Perhaps wisely, they tend to use it as a reward. Nonetheless, development by-products occur sufficiently often that reasonable encouragement of this kind of activity is desirable. The manager increases the probability of individual growth by displaying an interest in the organization's activities or the conference program and asking for information about new concepts and the employee's thoughts about applying what he has learned to his work. In so doing, the manager makes it clear that he expects useful learning to result.

Self-Actualization

Suppose the employee has established a basic philosophy of life for himself leading to a definite structure of values, analyzed his capabilities, reached certain conclusions about his growth possibilities, and taken steps to increase his knowledge in contributing areas. Then what? How does he go about implementing the personal plans that he will have formulated by now?

Fulfillment through work. At this point, the employee almost certainly looks to his work to help him implement his personal plans. He must find ways of doing this, not at the expense of the organization with which he is associated, but so that its results are, in fact, enhanced by the pursuit of his own interests. He asks himself, in effect, the question originally posed by the philosopher Robert Hartmann: "Assuming that I choose to remain in this organization, how can I *help* it to fulfill my meaning and my purpose in the world?"[4]

Too theoretical? Too intangible? Not at all. Consider the specialist in optics who is hired by a rocket firm

4 As quoted in Hoslett, *op. cit.*

to solve some very specific optical problems. Once these
are disposed of, his work is run-of-the-mine. A number
of choices follow: The specialist can leave because the
work is no longer challenging. The manager can try
to steer the man toward other fields, or can cut his pay
because the quality of his contribution is no longer very
great, or can overpay him to compensate for hiring him

Organizing Development Tools
III. *Around the Individual*

Development Goals	
Influence	
Inputs for Personal Goals	Professional Counseling Self-Analysis Managerial Feedback Computer Feedback

Increased Knowledge
and Skill
	Reading
	Training and Education
	    Programmed Learning,
	      Teaching Machines,
	      Programmed Texts
	    Simulation, Role Playing,
	      In-Basket, Business
	      Games
	    Case Study and Discussion
	Professional Organizations

Self-Actualization	Through Work
	    Self-Direction
	    Self-Measurement
	Through Community and Other
	    Outside Activities

in the first place. If the specialist really wants to work in optics, any one of these solutions is unsatisfactory. Sound goal negotiation in this case requires a real effort by the employee to identify needed contributions his specialized knowledge can make to the rocket business. This means thorough preparation as well as discussion with other professionals and perhaps with customers about important optical problems. It may require an invention or one or more innovative ideas. But the *opportunity* exists for the specialist to seek ways to contribute to the business and at the same time advance his career. Obviously, depending on the situation, he may not be able to suggest any further contributions he might make, or his manager may weigh all his suggestions and decide they would not be profitable. The specialist may have to leave to pursue his career.

Fortunately, the situation is seldom so extreme. For instance, the employee may be working as an individual contributor and may wish to develop supervisory or managing skills. Logically enough, he will negotiate to get into his work plans some specific goals which involve broader planning, short-term supervision, or better communicating skills. These are much easier for manager and organization to accommodate.

What is next in importance to self-direction is self-measurement. The development-minded manager therefore encourages each employee to develop standards by which he can judge himself. He supports the employee by asking for an evaluation of progress and personal effectiveness whenever they review the work together. He influences the employee toward standards of excellence by discussing the need for them frankly, exploring the reasons for differences of opinion between them, and stressing the importance of a factual objective look at results as they compare with the planned performance.

The trend toward self-measurement reinforces the close relationship between work and that implementation of personal goals which is becoming so important in today's changing work climate.

Fulfillment through community and other outside activities. For the most part, "extracurricular" activities are of an employee's own choosing; it is up to him to build them into his personal plans as he likes. Businesses today, however, frequently encourage employee participation in political, charitable, and similar community endeavors—either on an individual basis or, where appropriate, as a representative of the firm. Thus a man may be asked to head up a hospital fund-raising drive, serve on a planning board in conjunction with local school personnel, or speak before various groups.

The motive for participation is usually an unselfish one, but there is every reason to capitalize on the development possibilities of charitable or civic work. As a rule, one's assignments in these activities provide excellent opportunities to practice communication skills, both written and oral, to learn more about teamwork in the sense of setting joint goals and devising plans for action with one's associates, and to develop general human relationships skills. In specialized instances, they may also improve budgeting, planning, problem-solving, and decision-making skills and even—as in planning school curricula and working on conservation and civil defense projects—sharpen technical know-how.

Managers cannot count on outside activities to do their total development job for them, but it is certainly worth remembering that opportunities for development do exist outside the company and taking advantage of them in appropriate cases.

Responsible, Informed Self-Determination

Central to the whole concept of stimulating employee self-development is responsible, informed self-determination. Where the aim is development to achieve career goals, the employee has a great deal at stake. The effort and activity are his; the motive is his. Much of the information about his capability and all of the decisions about balance in his personal life come from him. For these reasons, the manager encourages as much self-determination on the job as is consistent with the employee's maturity, experience, and record of accomplishment. Thus employee self-determination is perhaps the manager's most powerful development tool.

If, however, the manager is to fulfill his responsibilities to the firm as well as to the employee, he cannot use self-determination for development purposes without considerable preparation and "homework." To permit the employee to devise his own work goals is an ideal way both to generate interest in his work and to capitalize on it. But the fact that these goals must serve the firm and help meet the organization's commitments places an enormous burden on the manager. He must supply enough information about company plans, the competitive situation, business strategy, and the like that the employee makes his choices from among legitimate alternatives.

To give the employee considerable freedom in choosing how he will meet his goals is surely developmental, but his plans must tie in with selected work and be made in full knowledge of limitations that may exist with respect to financing, manpower, and other resources. To encourage the employee to obtain information about how well a certain piece of work filled customer requirements, so that he can adapt his plans and behavior to getting better results next time, is highly desirable as long as employee and manager have previously agreed on the criteria for judging success. Otherwise the employee may be misled by isolated or too heavily weighted evidence. To permit the employee to design his own job and the way he will function in it will undoubtedly give him greater satisfaction provided he clearly understands the total organization, his mission in it, and the roles of others who are a part of it.

These precautions need not lessen the development possibilities of self-determination by any means. They simply highlight the preparations the manager must make, the prerequisites he must insure in order to encourage self-determination in a way that will have lasting benefit for the individual as well as meeting basic responsibilities to the firm.

CHAPTER X

OUTLINING THE PRESIDENT'S DEVELOPMENT JOB

E VEN THOUGH MANAGERS RECOGNIZE THE IMPORTANCE OF employee development, understand something of the process, and are aware of the means available to encourage it, they may not take action. None of us always does what he knows he should do. For this human reason, if for no other, our discussion of the manager's role in employee development would be incomplete without at least a summary of the essential contribution made by the president or chief executive officer (in large companies, it may be the general manager of a particular division or subdivision). There are two basic steps he must take: The first is to define the development results he expects managers throughout the firm to achieve, and the second is to establish administrative systems which will facilitate the achievement of those results and demonstrate his clear intention that they be achieved. Both steps are critical; without them, it is unlikely that managers will view employee development as a high-priority responsibility.

Managers are usually not educators. If they had wanted to teach, they would probably have chosen the academic rather than the business world. Yet, when a company asks its managers to undertake responsibility for employee development, it is asking them to become educators, to help employees to learn and to apply what they learn, to present them with work situations in which they have almost no alternative except to learn. But, if development is thought of as an educational program, it is almost automatically set apart from "the real job," considered an "extra"—the first thing on *tomorrow's* agenda.

With the president, therefore, lies the responsibility of portraying the need for development as a work requirement, not an adjunct to it. This means he must believe in it. He must see clearly the relationship between better managing and better work and between better work and individual growth.

Setting Companywide Development Goals

The president's starting point, just as in all his work, is his business planning. He sets corporate objectives, strategies for meeting them, the basic course of action, and a rough timetable. Note that these are *not* development goals and plans. They are hard-core business plans by which the work of all concerned is to be guided. The president doesn't formulate them by himself, of course. He uses normal information channels, whatever staff assistance is available to him, the usual methods for examining alternatives and involving key employees. When the necessary decisions have been made and broad strategies agreed upon, they are in turn translated into more specific plans for implementation at successive levels by the various departments. For each organizational component, then, there is a specific body of work required.

The primary development target for each manager is

to help employees develop capabilities that will permit them to meet their share of the organization's commitments. Managers work toward this goal by all the means described in this book: making work as developmental as possible, creating a work climate which encourages innovation, and helping employees to recognize their talents, reassess their personal values, and apply both to doing their jobs more effectively.

A second development goal for each manager is, like the first, rooted in the overall business plans of the firm. It is concerned, however, not with the immediate translation of current commitments into expected contribution but, instead, with the longer-range prediction of the business's future needs. This may take the form of future work which the manager and his department must prepare to handle, or it may mean providing manpower with specific technological or managing skills required elsewhere in the company. And, while a manager can take action on his own to meet employee development goals related to current commitments, he cannot do so for the longer range. Coordination among managers is essential.

Company Manpower Planning

The necessary coordination is assured through the company's manpower development plan, defining, as it does, the specific contributions required from each manager.

No president would expect to carry out projected business plans, much less persuade the board of directors to agree to them, without having worked out their financing. In just the same way, business plans cannot be considered acceptable until a way of providing needed manpower has been evolved. Certain technological skills are scarce, innovative talent is hard to find, inadequate managing skill is limiting the ability of many companies to grow at projected rates. The old attitude that "we'll decide what we want to do and then we'll hire the people we need to do it" is no longer sound. Included in "what we want to do" should be a scheme for developing the manpower required to do it.

The first steps in building such a manpower plan are systematic appraisals of (1) manpower needs and their timing as required by business plans and (2) current manpower capability and projected manpower trends. A comparison of these two leads to firm goals for specialized recruiting, training, and individual employee development, and these in turn require an analysis of the required investment. If it is too great, and less expensive methods of financing cannot be found, the manpower goals may have to be re-established on a more economically justifiable basis. Or, if the likelihood of achieving the manpower goals is small, regardless of the cost in dollars or effort, the business plans also may need modification. In any event, once interaction between business and manpower planning has produced goals that are compatible with each other and appear realistic, the mapower plans are interpreted for each organizational component just as are the business plans. Each manager, including the chief executive, undertakes responsibility for meeting his defined share of the goals.

Because both business and manpower plans are based on assumptions about future events, the president or chief executive reviews them frequently and adjusts them on the basis of current trends. As an example, suppose the head of a downtown department store makes plans to open a series of small suburban shops during the next 10 to 20 years. On the business side of the ledger, he predicts the potential volume of the small shops and the possible loss to the downtown store. If it seems that the result will be worth the investment, he and his staff proceed to develop more accurate figures and sources of financing. They do market research to select the geographic areas that appear likely to attract the most desirable business. Also on the business side of the ledger—and this is not an afterthought, not a tangent, but an important part of their calculations—they look at the number of new employees it will take to man the expanded facilities. Is a branch manager needed for each store, or can one manager handle several shops? What about buying? Can it be done centrally, or will there be enough differences from shop to shop that the buying staff will need to be expanded? What about displays? Sales personnel? Should experienced downtown store personnel be moved to the branches? Where will their replacements come from? Clearly the downtown store must not be denuded of its talent.

Once tentative decisions have been reached on these and similar questions, the store manager must take a look at present manpower. Does it seem likely that replacements can be developed *in time* from within? Are there shortages which will require specific recruiting efforts? What special training will have to be offered to accelerate employee readiness? Will the training staff itself have to be augmented and trained in order to give new recruits, particularly in the sales area, introductory and continuing training on an efficient basis? How much lead time is needed?

In most cases, the top man does not do all the work of data collection and analysis himself. He does, however, take the lead in making sure that every business plan is supported by a sound manpower plan, that all plans are implemented, and that they are kept current.

There are a number of tools available for comparing present manpower with projected needs.

Personnel inventory or register. The individual personnel file is not a particularly efficient way in which to look at manpower information on a group basis or even to search for particular skills or talents. However, mechanical inventory systems which call for the coding of basic factual information, such as age, education, experience, and skills, have been on the increase for more than twenty years and may be adequate for small businesses. And modern high-speed electronic data processing equipment is a decided asset to large companies in keeping track of toolmakers, welders, managers, engineers and scientists of specific kinds, and so on; for locating unusual skills or combinations of skills (a thermodynamicist who speaks Hungarian or a labor relations expert familiar with Brazilian law, for example); and for predicting ages, salary costs, and the like for various groups and occupations at a given point in time.

Manning and turnover tables; statistical projections. A projection of the current organization into the critical years is helpful for planning purposes. For the manager group, age distribution projected to certain dates, with due allowance for expected turnover because of resignations, retirements, and deaths as well as general mobility and promotions, gives an estimate of what specific positions will have to be filled at what approximate dates. For the general employee group, a similar analysis, focusing on skills rather than specific positions, provides a basis for likely recruiting and training needs. The additional or changed requirements anticipated by business plans must also be taken into account and the total picture studied for ways and means of meeting them. Obviously, when a large volume of data is involved, a mechanical or electronic data processing system is useful.

Managers' recommendations. The more judgmental sort of information about employees—predictions of behavior change, of rate of talent increase, of new-skill acquisition, of ability to do a different kind of work— probably is most satisfactorily obtained at the present time by asking managers for their evaluations. Because these are necessarily subjective and suffer from lack of uniform standards or values as well as from the very natural desire not to hurt an employee's future, managers are usually asked to follow some sort of *ranking* device in order to identify the best current and potential performers for whatever position or task is being considered.

One such device, a relatively simple one, is to list employees in the order in which they are most likely to be able to assume supervisory responsibility, say, or do customer service work. When the various managers' lists are collected, the top several choices on each list (the exact number depends a great deal on existing needs) are reconciled, usually by the next higher-level manager. These make up a pool of likely employees who might be offered special broadening work or learning opportunities. The employees' identification is no guarantee of their advancement; it simply gives an idea of the talent on hand to fill identified needs in the manpower plan within the required time span.

The ranking technique as a method for obtaining managerial judgments has, of course, numerous variations. "Straight" ranking requires the manager, starting at either end of the scale, to list all employees in the order in which he feels they can do or learn to do the task in question. *Alternate* ranking, as the name implies, calls for choosing the best individual and the poorest, then the second best and the second poorest, and so on until all are ranked. Managers usually find this a little easier than straight ranking, particularly if there are many employees to consider.

In *paired comparison,* each individual is compared with each other individual, and a choice is made as to which of the two is the better on each point in question. The individual chosen as "the better" the greatest number of times becomes No. 1 in the ranking; the one chosen the second greatest number of times becomes No. 2, and so on until the ranking is complete. This method again makes it a little easier to make choices among individuals provided the list of names is not too long.

A *forced choice* rating system is a professionally devised method whereby the person doing the rating chooses a statement which most nearly describes each employee, his behavior, or his work from among several which appear equally favorable or equally unfavorable. The replies are totaled by means of a pre-established weighting system, and from the totals a ranked list of employees is built up.

By whatever method managers make their recommendations, *collection by a trained specialist* sometimes serves a useful purpose. This is especially true if managers are making their evaluations for the first time or there is reason to believe that individual judgments vary considerably because of geographic separation, marked work differences, a tendency to rank "high" or "low," and the like. The specialist supplies, in effect, a common framework for managerial judgments. He sits with the manager while the latter reviews employees in turn, asks questions which draw out the reasons for judgments, and helps compare evidence about one employee's performance and estimated growth with the data on others. With his help the most promising employees for the position or task under consideration are identified and ranked. In short, he provides the reconciliation necessary to compile the list of individuals who eventually will make up the talent pool for specialized development efforts.

Assessment center. A few companies, in an attempt to supplement managers' judgments about employees who show growth capabilities in directions required by their business plans, have introduced a centrally administered assessment activity employing a wide variety of professional techniques.

> In appraising potentials in people today, possibly the most ambitious effort in all of industry is being made by the American Telephone and Telegraph Company. Its Assessment Center Program observes how selected employees behave under standardized conditions in order to determine their capacity for management. Patterned somewhat after the "situational" tests used by the Office of Strategic Services to select personnel during World War II, the AT&T approach puts close to 6,000 employees a year through a unique battery of tests, group exercises, work projects and stress situations. . . .
>
> Says Donald W. Bray, AT&T's director of personnel research: "To obtain as comprehensive a picture as can be had of men at the beginning of their careers in management, it is necessary to discover their abilities, aptitudes, goals, social skills and many other qualities. The most effective way of doing this, it appears to us, is to assemble the subjects, a few at a time, and have them spend several days together going through interviews, tests, group exercises and individual administrative work under the observation of a special staff."*

It should be obvious that none of these tools can be

---

* "The Hard Look in Employee Appraisal." Reprinted by special permission from *Dun's Review*, September 1966. Copyright, 1967, Dun & Bradstreet Publications Corporation.

used once and the resulting data frozen from that point forward. Information in personnel registers must reflect current abilities. Projections of manpower trends must incorporate the latest events. Managerial recommendations need frequent review so that lists of employees promotable to supervisory positions, for example, are adjusted as new evidence presents itself. Even judgments made as a result of an assessment-center approach need modification as individuals actually meet and handle real-life working situations. The manpower plan which supplies individual managerial goals for employee development is only as good as the information on which it is based, and the president's leadership is essential in keeping both business and related manpower plans current.

The President's Supporting Action

When business needs have been identified in manpower terms, when on-hand and potential talent have been reviewed, and when specific manpower requirements have been pinpointed, plans for recruitment, training, and individual learning must be drawn up and translated into the work of managers and specialists throughout the company. Supporting action is required from the president to insure that managers at each successive level in the organization will, in turn, work toward the development goals. The key elements of his support can be grouped into three categories: (1) formulation and communication of his philosophy of development and development's priority in the total work of the firm, (2) his personal example in carrying out his part of the company's development plans, and (3) the resources he provides for handling development work.

President's philosophy. A philosophy is a set of beliefs and attitudes about something. It is so much a part of the person that it permeates what he thinks, says, and does. In the development area the president of a company needs to think through what he believes about employee growth, its proper place in the work of the company, and his personal responsibility for its encouragement. He needs to put it into words for himself *in a practical fashion,* one which lends itself to action. Of necessity, it will vary with the president, with the firm, perhaps with the times, but it will undoubtedly include something like this: "One condition for a healthy business is that every employee, including me, by applying his full talent in his work, have the opportunity to add to his capabilities on a continuing basis, and be encouraged to do so. Moreover, business growth is dependent in large measure on individual growth. ..." Such a philosophy makes it clear that employee development is a part of managerial work to be implemented in the same way as all other work; that is, it requires specific, measurable, agreed-upon goals with established priorities, supported by specific tasks with due dates, progress reviewed at frequent intervals, and goals renegotiated with those concerned so as to reflect current situations.

Having formulated his personal philosophy of development and determined its current priority in managerial work, a president communicates his feelings and decisions in his speeches, both inside and outside the company, in his *off-the-cuff* comments in meetings with associates and employees throughout the firm, and in appropriate *company publications.* But another powerful vehicle for transmitting his basic philosophy is through *training programs* established for managers or potential managers at all organization levels. Such programs permit exploration of the philosophy with a view to understanding its implications for individual managerial action, along with the fundamental issues underlying it and the various possible approaches to developing the needed skills. A president will not plan or do the training in person except, perhaps, in very small firms. However, his interest should extend to insuring that there *is* high-quality manager training available, if necessary by an outside agency, and that it reflects his thinking and the importance he places on employee development in the total work of a manager.

Personal example. It is seldom enough to state a belief; demonstration carries more weight. A development-minded president needs to meet his part of the company's development goals, beginning with the vice presidents and others who report to him. As for any manager, his primary goal is improved performance on current work; beyond that there is his needed contribution to the firm's manpower plan. And all the concepts, tools, and approaches discussed in earlier chapters are available to him. Is the work of each person conducive to development? Is the president helping to reinforce the learning that comes from doing it? Is he setting a climate which encourages innovation to an extent consistent with business objectives? Is he promoting self-development? Is he providing special learning experiences which are leading individuals in the directions of growth required by the company's plans?

The president needs to devote much time and thought specifically to the development of his successor and of successors to those managers who report to him. Here is a problem that is largely outside the scope of this book, yet the involvement of all likely individuals in the work of the president is certainly a vital step. The development-minded president deliberately makes his work visible, shares his difficulties, and asks for the help of employees who currently (or potentially may) report to him. He draws them into data collection, data analysis, and decision making. He solicits their proposals for evolving and formulating company policy. Why? He does all this for two reasons: He wants them to grow in their understanding of the business, and he also needs the benefit of their contribution and their later influence in implementing the decisions made.

When the president fills a position directly below his own, he considers the candidates' employee development record as well as their profit results. He seeks specific evidence of outstanding individuals brought into the firm, individuals contributed to other parts of the company, employee mobility in the departments managed, and other evidence that these men have consciously encouraged employee development. Furthermore, he applies the same principles in appraising candidates to fill a position two organization levels below himself.

A president goes about displaying his continuing interest in development in many ways. He asks who is responsible for outstanding pieces of work and, whenever he can, he tries to meet that person. He looks at data on turnover, mobility, and promotions in and out of departments and asks questions to find out the reasons for them. When he visits geographically separated plants, he creates situations for meeting key personnel and talking to them. He routinely meets new, promising individuals brought into the firm in important positions.

The president sets the pattern for reward in the firm. If he rewards short-term results only, all the philosophy in the world won't take the focus off today's problems and their solution. He is therefore in the position of finding the proper point of balance between the long and the short range. Since situational factors may change this point for the entire company or, more often, cause it to shift in one area, the results expected over a five- or ten-year period, depending on the nature and status of the business, should be renegotiated annually. The president should take the lead in clarifying the current emphasis. For example, in a period of general economic crisis it may be possible to give only token effort to long-range goals while attention is necessarily focused on survival. In a young and growing business, on the other hand, the longer range may be stressed—rightly.

Does this mean that employee development should be allowed to suffer because of current conditions? Not at all. The opportunities to build development into existing work are always there—in fact, are heightened during periods of stress. Some of the "frills" may go: the more elaborate training programs, the more expensive adjuncts to information exchange such as banquets or meetings away from the plant or office. But the hard-core elements of work, climate, and individual talent and interest remain available for focusing on development. If compensation and non-monetary recognition correspond to the negotiated and agreed-upon development results, effort will soon be exerted to achieve those results.

Resources and Systems for Development

One further contribution still is required from the president: to supply the resources needed throughout the company if development work is to be effective. These resources include adequate funds, space, facilities, and competent personnel to help managers develop needed skills in themselves and in the employees who report to them.

Equally important are the systems which serve as

machinery for implementing development work. The most fundamental is a system of sound personnel practices: a selection system which improves the odds in matching talent and job requirements, an employee appraisal system designed to provide accurate information about performance and performance improvement, a promotion system which includes development needs and past development success in its criteria, training systems which encourage technical and management learning, and a compensation system which rewards successful development efforts. In addition, there are a number of management devices which are useful in making clear the president's intentions about development and which involve managers in evaluating their efforts toward their goals.

Committee, study, or task force. A manpower plan made in isolation by the president of the company with or without staff assistance, even of the most professional kind, may be hard to sell to those who must do the work. For their better understanding and their personal involvement, it is desirable to ask key employees to contribute information and ideas to any sort of overall company planning. Therefore, a committee or task force is often established to help formulate the manpower plan, to interpret it at various levels in the organization, to assist in reviewing progress, and to make suggestions for updating it in accordance with changes inside or outside the company. It is helpful if at least one member is a professional in the development process so that guidance is available in those areas of appraisal and action where technical knowledge and experience are required. Other members may be executives who report directly to the president or a mix of senior and junior executives and specialists. Membership may be either fixed or rotated on a yearly or bi-yearly basis in order to make the experi-

The President's Role in Employee Development

Areas of Responsibility	Tools and Approaches

Unification of Development Goals and Plans Stemming from Business Plans	Manpower Planning
	  Personnel Inventory or Register
	  Manning Tables, Turnover
	    Tables, Statistical
	    Projections
	  Managers' Recommendations
	    of Promotable Individuals
	  "Straight" Ranking
	  Alternate Ranking
	  Paired Comparisons
	  Collection by Specialist
	  Assessment Center

Supporting Action	Philosophy of Development,
	  Formulation and Communication
	  Speeches, Publications
	  Manager Training
	
	Personal Example
	  Development of Vice
	    Presidents
	  Presidential Visibility and
	    Receptivity
	  Development Priority in
	    Selection and Promotion
	    Decisions
	  Expressions of Sustained
	    Interest
	  Reward and Recognition for
	    Development
	
	Resources and Systems
	  Personnel, Funding, Space
	    and Equipment
	  Basic Personnel Practices
	  Manpower Development
	    Committee, Executive
	    Development Study, or
	    Task Force
	  Manpower Development
	    Reviews, Organization
	    Reviews
	  Development Surveys or Audits
	  Staff Assistance

ence available to as wide a circle of personnel as desired without sacrificing continuity of purpose and effort.

In large companies, such committees may be formed at headquarters and duplicated at the division or plant level.

Manpower or organization review. Another useful tool, particularly for evaluating progress against company manpower plans but also for stressing the on-going responsibility for improved performance in every position, is the manpower or organization review. Companies have various methods of handling it; the essential point is that, just as budget reviews are held at least annually, so manpower reviews should be held at about the same intervals. The manager in charge asks each manager who reports to him to project his organization structure a year ahead, on the basis of foreseeable work to be done, and to analyze the employees' current performance and future contribution in certain ways. It usually is more profitable if conclusions are presented orally and backed up by documented evidence. It also helps if a professional development "expert" is available to serve as a resource man for advice and suggestions in individual cases and to clarify appraisal and action plans through skillful questioning.

From the resulting discussion, plans for development of individual employees are made or revised, and group needs are identified which call for action by the personnel department or the manager himself. Needless to say, it is the careful follow-through, the year-after-year refinement of the plans made, which produces the ultimate payoff.

Surveys or audits. If development goals are specified for managers of each organization component and plans are developed for meeting them, an audit or review of progress may be made by a member of the personnel department, a specialist or team of specialists from headquarters, or an outside consultant. So that managerial energy won't be spent on fighting reported results or hiding inadequacies in performance, it is usually wise to involve managers in the collection and presentation of evidence, to invite their participation in analyzing the data, and to focus their attention on replanning to meet goals more effectively.

Staff assistance. In the headquarters organization and at various other levels in the company, depending on its size, a staff assistant may be needed to program specialized learning experiences for individuals. This is especially likely to be the case if these learning experiences take employees outside the jurisdiction of their managers and involve assignments in other parts of the company or in special task-force efforts which cross organization lines. The man who does this development programming often serves, also, as a consultant to the managers as they work toward their total development goals.

To ask for employee growth and fail to indicate the direction it can most usefully take, or to indicate that direction and fail to provide motivation, machinery, and resources for getting it done, is totally unrealistic. The president must accept his two-pronged responsibility for (1) sound manpower planning translated into individual managerial work and (2) personal action to implement his development philosophy, carry out his share of the manpower plan, and provide resources and systems for facilitating employee growth. Thus he gives impetus to the program and integrates the efforts of managers throughout the company so that their development work contributes directly to both short- and long-term business success.

CHAPTER XI

IMPLICATIONS—ETHICAL
CONSIDERATIONS—CAUTIONS

O NCE A MAN ACCEPTS RESPONSIBILITY FOR GETTING WORK done through other people, he faces a dual accountability. He is accountable for meeting the goals which are his share of the firm's business plans, and he is simultaneously accountable for the human results of his managing. These are not opposing management objectives. Rather, they must be linked in a sort of "marriage," so that the organization is staffed with individuals whose talents and interest match both current and foreseeable work needs reasonably well, work goals are set which use and challenge personal capabilities, and the organizational climate encourages innovation and personal growth.

It is, in fact, the interaction of these two concurrent responsibilities which is the essence of managing. The man who focuses solely on his work responsibility becomes a production expediter. If he focuses solely on human responsibilities, he is a teacher or counselor. Only when he brings both into balance is he managing. Job descriptions, supervisory and management training, organization goals and plans, measurement and compensation systems—all should reflect this fundamental truth.

The Counterbalance of Self-Determination

In outlining the manager's role in the development process, stressing the steps he should take and the tools and approaches available for his use, the managerial role may be overstated. The impression may be given that employee growth is subject to the manager's whim; that he is, in effect, planning careers and that the individual employee is at his mercy. This, of course, is not and should not be true. The manager is certainly an important factor in employees' occupational growth, for he assigns the work and provides or interprets the climate in which it is done. If he is astute, he capitalizes on employee talents and interests as well. And, since it is the favorable interaction of these factors which results in development, his role cannot be downgraded. But the employee's responsibility for his own development should be emphasized sharply and a better balance established between the two roles: the manager's on the one hand and the employee's on the other.

In a free society, an individual must inevitably accept responsibility for his decisions and actions. It is he, in the final analysis, regardless of influences, who selects his job and who consciously or unconsciously chooses each day to remain in it. It is he who copes with situations facing him in both his personal and his working life. He may do this constructively, literally wringing all the useful learning he can from them. Or he may rebel and either refuse to learn from experience or choose to ignore what he learns.

No individual is dependent on his manager for either the direction or the rate of his personal growth. At *best*, he is able to introduce into his work personal goals which involve doing something new, doing something in a better way, or applying it to a different kind of result. By the strength of his personality, he can set his own working climate, surrounding himself with an atmosphere for absorbing, innovating, and coping which can be as powerful as that created by any manager. By his choice of job and personal work standards, he can capitalize on his abilities. At *worst*, if he lacks the self-insight and confidence to do all this, and if help and encouragement are not forthcoming from his manager, he has the possibilities of continuing his education to increase his knowledge and skill, he can perhaps qualify through his own efforts for a higher-level job, and he has a host of family, church, and community activities as further outlets for self-expression.

No Manipulation of Careers

While some managers do too little in the development area, others overstep—or appear to overstep—legitimate ethical boundaries. Most people want to manage their own lives, and that includes their careers. They certainly understand the element of chance, which may favor them or not, but to the extent that they can be ready to seize opportunities or cope with bad luck, they like to be "in charge."

Managers should therefore avoid like the proverbial plague any resemblance to the chess player moving his men on the board or the puppet master manipulating his dolls on their strings. Growth is a freeing-up process, one which makes employees more independent of the manager, more able to act on their own, while recognizing at the same time the value of the information, resources, and systems he supplies. This is one of the reasons for insistence throughout this book on employee involvement in goal setting and the examination of alternate paths to goals even for prescribed work. It is one of the reasons for asking the manager to encourage the expression of differences of opinion, to permit the imposition of personal values on work required by the company, and to find upward channels for information and ideas that may influence the business for the better.

Fortunately the manager has a selfish motive for involving employees in this way—he badly needs their help to improve his decision-making ability.

Should Growth Possibilities Always Be Disclosed?

Should the employee invariably be informed by his manager of the direction in which he can hope to advance if he meets work or development goals? Not necessarily. In most cases, of course, the probabilities are apparent from the goal itself, and the employee's realization that he is being offered a real opportunity is distinctly useful. For, if people know what they are expected to achieve, they are more likely to achieve it; and, if they see managerial action as serving their interests, they are more likely to cooperate.

So, even if work may require the employee to grow considerably, the manager need not sit down and explain just how it is likely to affect the future course of the employee's career. If he sees benefits for the employee, he'll probably point them out. As a matter of fact, however, the manager usually does not know with any certainty what effect a given job will have on an individual; so there is little point in sharing his speculations. On the other hand, if he asks an employee to do something extra, something outside his scope of responsibility, or something which calls for unusual effort, he should in most cases explain the reasoning behind his request. Indeed, he has everything to gain by doing so.

Occasionally, managers create or use situations specifically to help the employee in personal ways. He may, for example, need to learn more acceptable behavior, acquire greater poise in meeting higher levels of managers or important customers, or become interested in fields with which he is quite unfamiliar or which he feels have nothing to offer him. How much to tell the employee in such cases is a delicate problem. If certain ways of handling the situation will bring credit to the employee, or if specific effort on the employee's part will be helpful, the manager will want to discuss the matter with him ahead of time. But, if awareness of his deficiencies will make the man more self-conscious, less sure of himself, the effect of his knowing just why he is being exposed to the big customer or the unfamiliar company function is likely to be unfavorable. The manager will do well to provide a minimum of advance explanation, although after the event he may want to help the employee reinforce whatever learning may have occurred. The issue is not a moral or ethical one, it is simply a matter of sensitive managerial judgment.

Basically, then, in most cases it is the employee's responsibility to analyze for himself the development implications of his work and make sure they are compatible with his personal interests and values. The manager should, however, capitalize on whatever advantages may be gained by making his own view of a particular opportunity explicit and stressing its possible effects during and after the completion of the work.

Insuring Career Continuity

The employee is responsible, too, for the continuity of his development. An individual reports to a number of managers in the course of his career, perhaps works in a number of firms or businesses, and the values and experiences of each of those managers are reflected in his development efforts. Some may contradict others; some may send him off on a tangent. The individual needs to focus continuously on his personal goals and values so as to smooth out these disjointed efforts. This doesn't mean he should choose as his target one ultimate job or one technological specialty and close his eyes to all others. Rather, his long-range focus should be broad, encompassing a range of possible future fields and positions. He must be free to capitalize on the favorable chance, the unusual opportunity.

The employee himself is the only one who can view his career as a whole and work within that framework.

The Dangers—and Uses—of Frankness

Just how frank should the manager be in discussing his personal estimate of an employee's future in the firm? This is an extraordinarily complex question, involving many human and ethical considerations. If the manager encourages the employee falsely, the employee may be misled into building up unwarranted expectations and making plans for the future which are unlikely to be fulfilled. The manager in this case is obviously out of bounds. His intentions are of little importance. He may have tried to be thoughtful and kind; the results, however, nullify the attempt.

But suppose, on the other hand, the manager misleads an employee in the opposite direction, paints the picture blacker than it is likely to be. If the employee is able but lacks self-confidence, perhaps has great untapped potential, he may simply give up trying and resign himself to 20 more years of the same unrewarding low-level job. It is hard to imagine why a manager might want to discourage an employee so thoroughly; but, whatever his intentions, the results are equally bad.

These, however, are deliberate falsifications which are clearly wrong. More difficult is the typical case in which the manager cannot know what the future holds—for the industry, for the firm, for the individual. All the evidence to date shows that his guesses about them individually and in toto are not likely to be very accurate. And so, with no deliberate intent to mislead, he may in fact do so. It is for this reason that discussions of potential are best kept within the framework of a next job or jobs or, even better, anticipated changes in the current job. Predictions then will be concerned with a time period sufficiently close that there should be enough evidence for sound forecasting.

If the employee insists on an opinion or even just speculation about his future with the firm because, for instance, he has had an offer from another company or hasn't had an increase in a long time, the manager should appraise the situation frankly, stating the basis for the conclusions reached and any assumptions made in reaching them. Then the employee can evaluate the manager's statements for himself.

Hazards in Managerial Deficiencies

For most individuals, early career influences appear to have the greatest impact. The work habits developed, the interests aroused, the self-confidence generated seem to stem most clearly from the first position and the first manager or supervisor. Too often this is unfortunate. Usually a man enters the working world at the bottom of the ladder. The manager or supervisor for whom he works is very likely to be either inexperienced himself, on his way up and just acquiring managerial skill and knowledge, or experienced but at or near his personal limits of growth. In neither case is he likely to summon up the level of managerial competence that encourages the kind of employee development companies need today or the early identification and utilization of outstanding talent.

A second handicap, one that persists throughout an individual's career, is that his manager's manager seldom has the opportunity to observe the manager in the act of managing. He sees the paper plan finally produced, but he cannot personally note the planning effort. He sees the completed appraisal form, but he cannot tune in on the judgment-making process or the appraisal session with the employee. He sees the work results, but he cannot watch the interpersonal relationships functioning.

Both these handicaps, which are probably not going to be eliminated very soon, point to the need for some distinctive planning to minimize hazards. A manager at one level in the organization should deliberately create situations which give him direct access to the work and thinking of the men two levels below him. He may, for example, occasionally hold staff meetings or round-tables on an enlarged basis. He may establish the practice of holding little work or business review sessions at which these employees two levels down speak for themselves. He may draw specific employees, regardless of organization position, into special studies and task forces or assign special problems for them to solve personally.

A second necessity is the use of tools like the attitude survey to alert the "manager's manager" to both favorable and unfavorable conditions; the employment of special consultants from inside or outside the organization, not only to assist him on both technical and personal matters but, in addition, to alert him to talent lower in the organization which is not being fully challenged; and, of course, channels of upward communication which are kept open and are independent of the normal organization hierarchy.

Finally, there must be training and education for all managers and supervisors so that their standards are continuously renewed and upgraded and sound interpersonal skills reinforced. Such training is needed, also, for the employees who report to these men, so that they too can improve their knowledge and abilities and exhibit their talents at least in a classroom situation. Classroom accomplishment can be made a matter of record so that inconsistency between grades and work performance can be examined to determine the reasons and suitable action taken when desirable.

Needed: Periodic Self-Evaluation

Although higher-level managers may take these precautions to assure that human talent is not buried or lost to the organization, supervisors and managers at all levels should be alerted to their personal responsibility for periodic evaluation of their interpersonal relationships and their ability to use development tools and approaches effectively. This means watching for employee reaction and exploring the reasons for it—good and bad.

No tool works for all people on all occasions. No system fits all individuals under all conditions. If a manager, for example, finds that his performance appraisal discussion with a certain employee arouses antagonism and defensiveness, and that performance afterward deteriorates rather than improves, he should take certain steps. He should first improve his knowledge and understanding of the appraisal process and ask himself whether the way he is handling it may not be leading to the unfavorable reaction. If possible, he should next seek professional help to upgrade his skill through training or personalized tutoring. If, after this, the employee still responds negatively, the manager should drop the customary appraisal discussion and try something else designed for the same purpose—perhaps employee self-appraisal or professional counseling.

If the unfavorable response comes only from one employee, the manager looks for a solution based on that employee's personal make-up or past experience. If, however, the response is more general, if he is forced to conclude that either his skill is at fault or the tool is not right for him, again he must stop using the tool and find another, more suitable one. This may seem obvious, but in many firms it is all too easy to follow the prescribed system and disclaim responsibility for results.

What the manager is responsible for, primarily, *is* results. If he cannot achieve them in the prescribed way, he must take the initiative and find a different way.

Let the Good Men Go!

One of the most irresponsible things a manager can do is try to "hold on" to his best men and, in so doing, fail to contribute talent which the company needs elsewhere in the organization. In the end he almost certainly loses the more capable employees since, failing to see opportunity for advancement within the company, they seek it elsewhere, perhaps with the firm's competitors. Moreover, he teaches people the bad habit of trying to best their manager rather than help him. Ultimately such a manager hurts himself most of all, for, except in times of economic depression when jobs are scarce, he ends up with a mediocre force, resentful at the lack of opportunity and willing to do only minimal work.

Let us face certain facts. When a manager does a good development job, when his organization earns a reputation for quality results on time, the employees reporting to him have frequent promotional opportunities. Indeed, the manager who really works at development will *seek* better jobs for those employees who he feels are ready for greater responsibilities. He invents ways to display their talents to others and bring their accomplishments to the attention of higher-level managers. The more capable men go on to bigger and better things; those who are less able leave for more suitable jobs elsewhere.

Although this high turnover places an inevitable hiring and training burden on the manager or supervisor, it also brings many benefits. The organization is eternally fresh; it looks at questions from many angles; it never develops an ingrown inflexibility about problem solutions. And, because the prospect of upward mobility is attractive to capable employees, staffing presents no insuperable difficulties in the long run.

Moreover, the high proportion of "people" activity in his job prepares the manager himself for greater responsibilities. For, as is frequently pointed out, progress up the management ladder makes greater demands on interpersonal skills and increases the percentage of working time devoted to the organization's human resources.

Employee Development Presupposes
Mature Managers

The task of helping each member of the organization
to be as effective as possible, to develop his talents and
abilities and use them fully, has important implications
for the manager as a person. It implies that he is secure
enough, mature enough, not to view increasing competence in his organization as a threat to his own position. He cannot feel that each employee who reports
to him is competing with him and thus endangering
his status and career in the firm. This, in turn, implies
a reasonably objective view of himself, an acceptance of
his own abilities and limitations and a constructive attitude about their use in furthering his personal objectives.

Clearly, all managers do not have this degree of self-
insight. Sometimes professional advice may be of help.
Sometimes the manager's manager may be able to minimize self-concern by providing the necessary support.
But, on the whole, an individual who cannot overcome
or at least control his feelings of anxiety or jealousy as
he sees his employees become more and more effective
may find his future brighter in a nonmanagerial position.

Employee development is not for the faint-hearted.
The climate which must be established is a tough climate—a manager who feels too strongly the need to be
liked probably cannot provide it. Think back to your
school years. The popular teacher was generally the one
who gave the easy quizzes, the least homework. But
the teacher who stimulated the most learning, who asked
the most of you, whom you remember and admire today,
made you extend yourself to keep pace. So it is with
managers. Those who contribute the most to employee

development are those who so involve the employee in the aims of the organization that he expresses his constructive dissatisfaction with his contribution to the company's well-being by attempting more promising (though more difficult) goals and more rewarding (though more innovative) methods.

This puts the employee uncomfortably at risk. It puts the manager at risk as well. The development-minded manager needs the courage to take this risk.

DEVELOPMENT QUIZ
FOR MANAGERS

THIS QUIZ IS FOR YOUR PERSONAL USE. IT IS INTENDED TO help you survey your managing practices to see whether you are capitalizing on employee development opportunities. Read each question and then place a checkmark in the column which you feel is most appropriate.

	I Do This Well Enough	Needs Improvement But Not Now	Needs Improvement Now
1. Every employee who reports to me has a written position description and written work plans covering the most important goals I expect him to achieve during the next three months.			
2. Whenever I assign work or review work plans, I make sure there is some challenging new work for each employee.			
3. Every employee has one improvement goal; that is, one part of his work which he is trying to do better or which will produce a bigger contribution to the organization.			

	I Do This Well Enough	Needs Improvement But Not Now	Needs Improvement Now
4. I take pride in keeping each employee informed about the business, the plans of the department, any changes in company thinking, and similar matters, so that he can do his work intelligently.			
5. I frequently ask employees to suggest goals for their work, give their reasons for suggesting them, and make plans for meeting them.			
6. I encourage each employee to know who his customers are—that is, what individuals or groups receive his work—and whether they are satisfied with what they are getting from him or have suggestions for improving it.			
7. I ask each employee to evaluate his work periodically and discuss with me how it could contribute more to the business and what would make it more satisfying to him.			
8. I encourage employees to make a reasonable number of innovations, to experiment, to find better work methods.			
9. I have systems or machinery which encourages employees to air any disagreements they may have about technical or administrative matters, along with their reasons.			

	I Do This Well Enough	Needs Improvement But Not Now	Needs Improvement Now
10. I do everything I can to thank those who bring me bad news early and to receive it constructively; that is, to focus on correcting the situation.			
11. In filling open jobs I consider the candidates' longer-range development needs and their potential value to the firm along with their immediate qualifications.			
12. When I make a recommendation for a merit increase, I consider the employee's successful development efforts, for the people reporting to him and for himself, as a major factor in my decision.			
13. I have up-to-date information on how each employee hopes to build a career for himself.			
14. I have a written appraisal of each employee's talents, areas of deficiency, and changing capabilities as observed during the past three years.			
15. I have identified an "unknown" with each employee— that is, an area of work he has never tried, some field of knowledge he has not studied or read about, or a skill he has not had the opportunity to practice—and I have encouraged him to take steps to fill the gap insofar as doing so might be useful in advancing his career interests.			

	I Do This Well Enough	Needs Improvement But Not Now	Needs Improvement Now
16. No employee, except one about to retire, has been on the same job longer than five years.			
17. The manager to whom I report knows which employees I believe are promotable and what next jobs they are most likely to be able to fill competently and when.			
18. No one in the organization is on a job for which he is unsuited.			
19. I keep the work I'm doing and the work decisions I'm making visible to employees and often ask them for their thoughts and suggestions to help me do my job better.			
20. All indications from attitude surveys, comments during meetings, and similar communications show the employees are aware that I expect them to use their abilities fully and develop them as rapidly as possible so that our overall contribution to the firm is continuously enlarged in specific ways.			

When you have checked the column you feel is right in each case, circle the three points which you have noted as needing improvement now and which you feel would have the highest immediate payoff for your business. Build a short but specific action plan to improve in each area.

Goal 1:_____

_____

_____

_____

_____

Action to meet Goal 1:

	Who Will Take This Action?	Starting Date	Completion Date
Step 1._____			
_____			
Step 2._____			
_____			
Step 3._____			
_____			
Step 4._____			
_____			
Step 5._____			
_____			

Goal 2:_____

_____

_____

_____

_____

Action to meet Goal 2:

	Who Will Take This Action?	*Starting Date*	*Completion Date*
Step 1._____			
_____			
Step 2._____			
_____			
Step 3._____			
_____			
Step 4._____			
_____			
Step 5._____			
_____			

Goal 3:_____

_____

_____

_____

_____

Action to meet Goal 3:

	Who Will Take This Action?	Starting Date	Completion Date
Step 1._____			
_____			
_____			
Step 2._____			
_____			
_____			
Step 3._____			
_____			
_____			
Step 4._____			
_____			
_____			
Step 5._____			
_____			
_____			

DEVELOPMENT QUIZ FOR PRESIDENTS OR GENERAL MANAGERS

THIS QUIZ IS FOR YOUR PERSONAL USE. IT IS INTENDED TO help you survey your managing practices to see whether you are capitalizing on employee development opportunities. Read each question and then place a checkmark in the column which you feel is most appropriate.

	I Do This Well Enough	Needs Improvement But Not Now	Needs Improvement Now
1. I involve the men who report to me, as well as other key employees, in building business plans for the company.			
2. I personally see that key employees, wherever they may be located in the organization, are aware of current business plans and strategies and are acquainted with any major shifts in these plans and the reasons for them.			

211

	I Do This Well Enough	Needs Improvement But Not Now	Needs Improvement Now
3. In my three latest speeches or presentations, I stressed at least once the importance of each manager's taking positive action to encourage employees to use their full talents in their jobs and find opportunities which require growth. I made a point of outlining a few of the talents the company would need during the next five years.			
4. Our company provides training for managers and prospective managers, and this training includes employee development concepts and skills.			
5. The managers who report to me and those who, in turn, report to them are fully aware of our company's manpower development plans, and each understands the specific employee development goals he is expected to achieve.			
6. I have a philosophy of employee development which I believe is right for our business and which managers in the firm know and can readily translate into practical action. It is in writing and has been discussed in public at least once in the past six months.			

	I Do This Well Enough	Needs Improve- ment But Not Now	Needs Improve- ment Now
7. If a manager anywhere in the firm feels the need for development information or advice, there is available to him a trained individual or organization for this purpose, and he knows how to go about getting the help he wants.			
8. Among the business results I regularly review are data on promotions, turnover, key personnel additions by name, employee appraisals completed, promotable employees, and similar information. The statistics included are published for use by our top managers.			
9. One factor on which I regularly appraise our executives is their record on employee development, and I take this into account in my compensation decisions.			
10. I have a manager development specialist to whom I look for advice and who helps me devise developmental experiences for unusually capable employees who need them.			
11. All those who report to me helped put together the manpower development plan which supports our business plans, and they help review our progress against it and its adequacy for future needs.			

	I Do This Well Enough	Needs Improvement But Not Now	Needs Improvement Now
12. Within the past 12 months I have discussed with each person who reports to me the satisfaction he gets from his work, the things he is learning, his ideas for self-improvement, and his current career targets.			
13. I often assign different aspects of problems affecting our business to promising employees for investigation and ask for their recommendations even though their position responsibilities may not include the area in question and even though they may not report directly to me.			
14. I sometimes assign different sides of a question to different key employees so that we may consider major issues for and against a course of action before reaching our decision.			
15. I know personally the 25 employees who are considered most promising in the firm and have personally reviewed some of their work.			
16. I have studied the age projection of key employees over the next 10-year period and believe we have several good choices for each position which we anticipate will open during that time.			

	I Do This Well Enough	Needs Improvement But Not Now	Needs Improvement Now
17. I ask our managers to document the accomplishments of all employees regularly, and we have a system for quickly locating specialized talent wherever it may be in the company.			
18. I am satisfied that employees who display promise of, and interest in, advancement do not remain in the same job for too long a time, and I have a system for checking on this point.			
19. Whenever I review business results, I also review progress in meeting development goals, and I do not consider any business to be healthy unless the men who are in it are growing in needed directions and at needed rates.			
20. I am personally on target in meeting the employee development goals which are my share of the company's manpower development plans.			

When you have checked the column which you feel is right in each case, circle the three points which you have noted as needing improvement now and which you feel would have the highest immediate payoff for your business. Build a short but specific action plan to improve in each area.

Goal 1:_____

_____

_____

_____

_____

Action to meet Goal 1:

	Who Will Take This Action?	Starting Date	Completion Date
Step 1._____			
_____			
_____			
Step 2._____			
_____			
_____			
Step 3._____			
_____			
_____			
Step 4._____			
_____			
_____			
Step 5._____			
_____			

Goal 2:_____

_____

_____

_____

_____

Action to meet Goal 2:

	Who Will Take This Action?	Starting Date	Completion Date
Step 1._____			
_____			
_____			
Step 2._____			
_____			
_____			
Step 3._____			
_____			
_____			
Step 4._____			
_____			
_____			
Step 5._____			
_____			
_____			

Goal 3:_____

_____

_____

_____

_____

Action to meet Goal 3:

	Who Will Take This Action?	Starting Date	Completion Date
Step 1._____			
_____			
_____			
Step 2._____			
_____			
_____			
Step 3._____			
_____			
_____			
Step 4._____			
_____			
_____			
Step 5._____			
_____			
_____			

INDEX